Sams **Teach Yourself**

Microsoft®

SQL Server
T-SQL

in **10**
Minutes

SAMS | 800 East 96th Street, Indianapolis, Indiana, 46240 USA

Sams Teach Yourself Microsoft® SQL Server T-SQL in 10 Minutes

Trademarks

Warning and Disclaimer

Bulk Sales

Sams Publishing offers excellent discounts on this book when ordered in quantity for bulk purchases or special sales. For more information, please contact

**U.S. Corporate and Government Sales
1-800-382-3419
corpsales@pearsontechgroup.com**

For sales outside of the U.S., please contact

**International Sales
international@pearsoned.com**

Acquisitions Editors
Loretta Yates
Damon Jordon

Development Editor
Mark Renfrow

Managing Editor
Patrick Kanouse

Project Editor
Mandie Frank

Copy Editor
Bart Reed

Indexer
WordWise Publishing Services, LLC.

Proofreader
Elizabeth Scott

Technical Editor
Jon Price

Publishing Coordinator
Vanessa Evans

Designer
Gary Adair

Table of Contents

About the Author

Ben Forta is Adobe Systems's Senior Technical Evangelist and has over 20 years of experience in the computer industry in product development, support, training, and product marketing. Ben is the author of the best-selling *Sams Teach Yourself SQL in 10 Minutes* (now in its third edition, and translated into more than a dozen languages), *MySQL Crash Course*, *ColdFusion Web Application Construction Kit* and *Advanced ColdFusion Development* (both published by Que), *Sams Teach Yourself Regular Expressions in 10 Minutes*, as well as books on Flash, Java, WAP, Windows 2000, and other subjects. He has extensive experience in database design and development, has implemented databases for several highly successful commercial software programs, and is a frequent lecturer and columnist on Internet and database technologies. Born in London, England, and educated in London, New York, and Los Angeles, Ben now lives in Oak Park, Michigan with his wife Marcy and their seven children. Ben welcomes your email at ben@forta.com, and invites you to visit his website at http://www.forta.com/.

Acknowledgments

First of all, I'd like to thank the folks at Sams for once again granting me the flexibility and freedom to build this book as I saw fit. Thanks to Mark Renfrow for once again providing invaluable and thorough feedback. Special thanks to Loretta Yates, Damon Jordan, and Mark Taber for bravely stepping in midstream and helping get this book back on track despite all of the changes and delays.

Thanks to Jon Price, one of the most thorough technical editors I have had the privilege of working with yet.

And finally, this book (as well as my *MySQL Crash Course*) is based on my *Sams Teach Yourself SQL in 10 Minutes*. The feedback that that book received is gratefully appreciated, and this volume is the result of many of your suggestions. Thank you, and I hope I have lived up to your expectations.

We Want to Hear from You!

As the reader of this book, *you* are our most important critic and commentator. We value your opinion and want to know what we're doing right, what we could do better, what areas you'd like to see us publish in, and any other words of wisdom you're willing to pass our way.

You can email or write me directly to let me know what you did or didn't like about this book, as well as what we can do to make our books stronger.

Please note that I cannot help you with technical problems related to the topic of this book, and that due to the high volume of mail I receive, I might not be able to reply to every message.

When you write, please be sure to include this book's title and author as well as your name and phone or email address. I will carefully review your comments and share them with the author and editors who worked on the book.

Email: opensourcefeedback@samspublishing.com

Mail: Mark Taber
          Associate Publisher
          Sams Publishing
          800 East 96th Street
          Indianapolis, IN 46240 USA

Reader Services

Visit our website and register this book at www.samspublishing.com/register for convenient access to any updates, downloads, or errata that might be available for this book.

This book also has a companion website at http://www.forta.com/books/0672328674. Visit this site for errata, downloads, a support forum, and more.

Introduction

Microsoft® SQL Server has become one of the most popular database management systems in the world. From small development projects to some of the best-known and most prestigious sites on the Web, SQL Server has proven itself to be a solid, reliable, fast, and trusted solution to all sorts of data-storage needs.

This book is based on my best-selling book *Sams Teach Yourself SQL in 10 Minutes*, which has become one of the most-used SQL tutorials in the world, with an emphasis on teaching what you really need to know, methodically, systematically, and simply. But as popular and as successful as that book is, it does have some limitations:

▶ In covering all the major DBMSs, coverage of DBMS-specific features and functionality had to be kept to a minimum.

▶ To simplify the SQL taught, the lowest common denominator had to be found; SQL statements that would (as much as possible) work with all major DBMSs. This requirement necessitated that better DBMS-specific solutions not be covered.

▶ Although basic SQL tends to be rather portable between DBMSs, more advanced SQL most definitely is not. As such, that book could not cover advanced topics, such as triggers, cursors, stored procedures, access control, transactions, and more in any real detail.

And that is where this book comes in. *Sams Teach Yourself Microsoft® SQL Server T-SQL in 10 Minutes* builds on the proven tutorials and structure of *Sams Teach Yourself SQL in 10 Minutes*, without getting bogged down with anything but Transact-SQL (T-SQL, for short). It starts with simple data retrieval and works on to more complex topics, including the use of joins, subqueries, full text-based searches, functions and stored procedures, cursors, triggers, table constraints, XML, and much more. You'll learn what you need to know methodically, systematically, and simply in highly focused lessons designed to make you immediately and effortlessly productive.

> NOTE: **Written for SQL Server 2005**
>
> This book was written with SQL Server 2005 in mind, and covers features and technologies new to that version of the software. However, with the exception of two lessons, the content and lessons can be used with earlier versions of SQL Server, including SQL Server 2000.

So turn to Lesson 1, "Understanding SQL," and get to work. You'll be taking advantage of all SQL Server has to offer in no time at all.

Who Is This Book For?

This book is for you if...

- ► You are new to SQL.

- ► You are just getting started with SQL Server and want to hit the ground running.

- ► You want to quickly learn how to get the most out of SQL Server and T-SQL.

- ► You want to learn how to use T-SQL in your own application development.

- ► You want to be productive quickly and easily using SQL Server without having to call someone for help.

Companion Website

This book has a companion website online at http://forta.com/books/ 0672328674/.

Visit the site to access the following:

- Table creation and population scripts used to create the sample tables used throughout this book

- The online support forum

- Online errata (should one be required)

- Other books that may be of interest to you

Conventions Used in This Book

This book uses different typefaces to differentiate between code and regular English, and also to help you identify important concepts.

Text that you type and text that should appear on your screen is presented in monospace type. It looks like this to mimic the way text looks on your screen.

Placeholders for variables and expressions appear in *monospace italic* font. You should replace the placeholder with the specific value it represents.

This arrow (➡) at the beginning of a line of code means that a single line of code is too long to fit on the printed page. Continue typing all the characters after the ➡ as though they were part of the preceding line.

> NOTE: A note presents interesting pieces of information related to the surrounding discussion.

> TIP: A tip offers advice or teaches an easier way to do something.

> CAUTION: A caution advises you about potential problems and helps you steer clear of disaster.

> **PLAIN ENGLISH:**   New Term icons provide clear definitions of new, essential terms.

Input ▼

Input identifies code that you can type in yourself. It usually appears next to a listing.

Output ▼

Output highlights the output produced by running T-SQL code. It usually appears after a listing.

Analysis ▼

Analysis alerts you to the author's line-by-line analysis of input or output.

LESSON 1

Understanding SQL

In this lesson, you'll learn about databases and SQL, prerequisites to learning T-SQL.

Database Basics

The fact that you are reading this book indicates that you, somehow, need to interact with databases. So before diving into SQL Server and its T-SQL implementation of the SQL language, it is important that you understand some basic concepts about databases and database technologies.

Whether you are aware of it or not, you use databases all the time. Each time you select a name from your email address book, you are using a database. If you conduct a search on an Internet search site, you are using a database. When you log into your network at work, you are validating your name and password against a database. Even when you use your ATM card at a cash machine, you are using databases for PIN verification and balance checking.

But even though we all use databases all the time, there remains much confusion over what exactly a database is. This is especially true because different people use the same database terms to mean different things. Therefore, a good place to start our study is with a list and explanation of the most important database terms.

> TIP: **Reviewing Basic Concepts**
> What follows is a very brief overview of some basic database concepts. It is intended either to jolt your memory, if you already have some database experience, or to provide you with the absolute basics, if you are new to databases. Understanding databases is an important part of mastering SQL Server and T-SQL, and you might want to find a good book on database fundamentals to brush up on the subject if needed.

What Is a Database?

The term *database* is used in many different ways, but for our purposes a database is a collection of data stored in some organized fashion. The simplest way to think of it is to imagine a database as a filing cabinet. The filing cabinet is simply a physical location to store data, regardless of what that data is or how it is organized.

> PLAIN ENGLISH: **Database**
> A container (usually a file or set of files) to store organized data.

> CAUTION: **Misuse Causes Confusion**
> People often use the term *database* to refer to the database software they are running. This is incorrect, and it is a source of much confusion. Database software is actually called the *Database Management System* (or DBMS). The database is the container created and manipulated via the DBMS. A database might be a file stored on a hard drive, but it might not. And for the most part, this is not even significant because you never access a database directly anyway; you always use the DBMS, and it accesses the database for you.

Tables

When you store information in your filing cabinet, you don't just toss it in a drawer. Rather, you create files within the filing cabinet, and then you file related data in specific files.

In the database world, that file is called a *table*. A table is a structured file that can store data of a specific type. A table might contain a list of customers, a product catalog, or any other list of information.

PLAIN ENGLISH: **Table**

A structured list of data of a specific type.

The key here is that the data stored in the table is one type of data or one list. You would never store a list of customers and a list of orders in the same database table. Doing so would make subsequent retrieval and access difficult. Rather, you'd create two tables, one for each list.

Every table in a database has a name that identifies it. That name is always unique, meaning no other table in that database can have the same name.

NOTE: **Table Names**

What makes a table name unique is actually a combination of several things, including the database name and table name. This means that although you cannot use the same table name twice in the same database, you definitely can reuse table names in different databases.

Tables have characteristics and properties that define how data is stored in them. These include information about what data may be stored, how it is broken up, how individual pieces of information are named, and much more. This set of information that describes a table is known as a *schema*, and schemas are used to describe specific tables within a database, as well as entire databases (and the relationship between tables in them, if any).

PLAIN ENGLISH: **Schema**

Information about database and table layout and properties.

Columns and Datatypes

Tables are made up of columns. A column contains a particular piece of information within a table.

PLAIN ENGLISH: **Column**

A single field in a table. All tables are made up of one or more columns.

The best way to understand this is to envision database tables as grids, somewhat like spreadsheets. Each column in the grid contains a particular piece of information. In a customer table, for example, one column contains the customer number, another contains the customer name, and the address, city, state, and ZIP Code are all stored in their own columns.

TIP: **Breaking Up Data**

It is extremely important to break data into multiple columns correctly. For example, city, state, and ZIP Code should always be separate columns. By breaking these out, it becomes possible to sort or filter data by specific columns (for example, to find all customers in a particular state or in a particular city). If city and state are combined into one column, it would be extremely difficult to sort or filter by state.

Each column in a database has an associated datatype. A datatype defines what type of data the column can contain. For example, if the column is to contain a number (perhaps the number of items in an order), the datatype would be numeric. If the column were to contain dates, text, notes, currency amounts, and so on, the appropriate datatype would be used to specify this.

PLAIN ENGLISH: **Datatype**

A type of allowed data. Every table column has an associated datatype that restricts (or allows) specific data in that column.

Datatypes restrict the type of data that can be stored in a column (for example, preventing the entry of alphabetical characters into a numeric field). Datatypes also help sort data correctly, and they play an important role in optimizing disk usage. As such, special attention must be given to picking the right datatype when tables are created.

Rows

Data in a table is stored in rows; each record saved is stored in its own row. Again, envisioning a table as a spreadsheet-style grid, the vertical columns in the grid are the table columns, and the horizontal rows are the table rows.

For example, a customers table might store one customer per row. The number of rows in the table is the number of records in it.

> PLAIN ENGLISH: **Row**
> A record in a table.

> NOTE: **Records or Rows?**
> You might hear users refer to database *records* when referring to *rows*. For the most part, the two terms are used interchangeably, but *row* is technically the correct term.

Primary Keys

Every row in a table should have some column (or set of columns) that uniquely identifies it. A table containing customers might use a customer number column for this purpose, whereas a table containing orders might use the order ID. An employee list table might use an employee ID or the employee Social Security number column.

PLAIN ENGLISH: **Primary Key**

A column (or set of columns) whose values uniquely identify every row in a table.

This column (or set of columns) that uniquely identifies each row in a table is called a *primary key*. The primary key is used to refer to a specific row. Without a primary key, updating or deleting specific rows in a table becomes extremely difficult because there is no guaranteed safe way to refer to just the rows to be affected.

TIP: **Always Define Primary Keys**

Although primary keys are not actually required, most database designers ensure that every table they create has a primary key so future data manipulation is possible and manageable.

Any column in a table can be established as the primary key, as long as it meets the following conditions:

▶ No two rows can have the same primary key value.

▶ Every row must have a primary key value (primary key columns may not allow NULL values).

NOTE: **Primary Key Rules**

The rules listed here are enforced by SQL Server itself.

Primary keys are usually defined on a single column within a table. But this is not required, and multiple columns may be used together as a primary key. When multiple columns are used, the rules previously listed must apply to all columns that make up the primary key, and the values of all columns together must be unique (individual columns need not have unique values).

> TIP: **Primary Key Best Practices**
>
> In addition to the rules that SQL Server enforces, several universally accepted best practices should be adhered to:
>
> - Don't update values in primary key columns.
> - Don't reuse values in primary key columns.
> - Don't use values that might change in primary key columns. (For example, when you use a name as a primary key to identify a supplier, you would have to change the primary key when the supplier merges and changes its name.)

There is another very important type of key called a *foreign key*, but I'll get to that later on in Lesson 14, "Joining Tables."

What Is SQL?

SQL (pronounced as the letters *S-Q-L* or as *sequel*) is an abbreviation for Structured Query Language. SQL is a language designed specifically for communicating with databases.

Unlike other languages (spoken languages, such as English, or programming languages, such as Java or Visual Basic), SQL is made up of very few words. This is deliberate. SQL is designed to do one thing and do it well: provide you with a simple and efficient way to read and write data from a database.

What are the advantages of SQL?

- SQL is not a proprietary language used by specific database vendors. Almost every major DBMS supports SQL, so learning this one language enables you to interact with just about every database you'll run into.

- SQL is easy to learn. The statements are all made up of descriptive English words, and there aren't that many of them.

- Despite its apparent simplicity, SQL is actually a very powerful language, and by cleverly using its language elements you can perform very complex and sophisticated database operations.

> NOTE: **DBMS-Specific SQL**
>
> Although SQL is not a proprietary language and a standards commit-
> tee exists that tries to define SQL syntax that can be used by all
> DBMSs, the reality is that no two DBMSs implement SQL identically.
> The SQL taught in this book is T-SQL (Transact-SQL) and is specific
> to Microsoft SQL Server, and although much of the language taught
> will be usable with other DBMSs, do not assume complete SQL syn-
> tax portability.

Try It Yourself

All the lessons in this book use working examples, showing you the SQL
syntax, what it does, and explaining why it does it. I'd strongly suggest
that you try each and every example for yourself so as to learn T-SQL
first hand.

Appendix B, "The Example Tables," describes the example tables used
throughout this book, and explains how to obtain and install them. If you
have not done so, refer to this appendix before proceeding.

> NOTE: **You Need SQL Server**
>
> Obviously, you'll need access to a copy of SQL Server to follow
> along. Appendix A, "Getting Started with SQL Server," explains where
> to get a copy of SQL Server and provides some pointers for getting
> started. If you do not have access to a copy of SQL Server, refer to
> that appendix before proceeding.

Summary

In this first lesson, you learned what SQL is and why it is useful. Because
SQL is used to interact with databases, you also reviewed some basic
database terminology.

LESSON 2

Introducing SQL Server

In this lesson, you'll learn what SQL Server is and the tools you can use when working with it.

What Is SQL Server?

In the previous lesson, you learned about databases and SQL. As explained, it is the database software (*DBMS* or *Database Management System*) that actually does all the work of storing, retrieving, managing, and manipulating data. SQL Server is a DBMS; that is, it is database software.

SQL Server has been around for a long time and is in use at millions of installations worldwide. Why do so many organizations and developers use SQL Server? Here are some of the reasons:

- ▶ **Performance:** SQL Server is fast (make that *very* fast).

- ▶ **Trusted:** SQL Server is used by some of the most important and prestigious organizations and sites, all of whom entrust it with their critical data.

- ▶ **Integration:** SQL Server is tightly integrated with other Microsoft offerings.

- ▶ **Simplicity:** SQL Server is one of the easiest DBMSs to install and get up and running, and includes administrative tools that make management of the server painless and simple.

So why not use SQL Server? First and foremost, SQL Server only runs on Windows, and if your servers run other another operating system (such as Linux), then obviously you'll not be able to use SQL Server. In addition,

SQL Server is a commercial product, and for those interested in no-cost open-source offerings, other DBMSs may be more attractive. And finally, SQL Server has been criticized for not supporting high-end enterprise features (such as clustering and fault tolerance) as well as some other DBMSs, although this criticism has in many ways been addressed in SQL Server 2005.

Client Server Software

DBMSs fall into two categories: shared file–based and client/server. The former (which include products such as Microsoft Access and FileMaker) are designed for desktop use and are generally not intended for use on higher-end or more critical applications.

Databases such as SQL Server, Oracle, and MySQL are client/server–based databases. Client/server applications are split into two distinct parts. The *server* portion is a piece of software that is responsible for all data access and manipulation. This software runs on a computer called the *database server*.

Only the server software interacts with the data files. All requests for data, data additions and deletions, and data updates are funneled through the server software. These requests or changes come from computers running client software. The *client* is the piece of software with which the user interacts. If you request an alphabetical list of products, for example, the client software submits that request over the network to the server software. The server software processes the request; filters, discards, and sorts data as necessary; and sends the results back to your client software.

> NOTE: **How Many Computers?**
> The client and server software may be installed on two computers or on one computer. Regardless, the client software communicates with the server software for all database interaction, be it on the same machine or not.

All this action occurs transparently to you, the user. The fact that data is stored elsewhere or that a database server is even performing all this processing for you is hidden. You never need to access the data files directly.

In fact, most networks are set up so that users have no access to the data, or even the drives on which it is stored.

Why is this significant? Because to work with SQL Server, you'll need access to both a computer running the SQL Server software and client software with which to issue commands to SQL Server:

- ▶ The server software is the SQL Server DBMS. You can run a locally installed copy, or you can connect to a copy running on a remote server to which you have access.

- ▶ The client can be SQL Server–included tools, scripting languages (such as Perl), web application development languages (such as ASP, ASP.NET, ColdFusion, JSP, and PHP), programming languages (such as Visual Basic, VB.NET, C, C++, C#, and Java), and more.

SQL Server Versions

Client tools are revisited in a moment. First, a quick word about DBMS versions.

The current version of SQL Server is SQL Server 2005 (although SQL Server 2000 and prior versions are in use in many organizations). This book was written for SQL Server 2005, with SQL Server 2000 in mind as well (although much of the content will apply to prior versions as well).

TIP: **Use Version 2005**

If at all possible, the use of SQL Server 2005 is recommended. Not only will this make it possible for you to follow along with every lesson in this book (including two lessons specific to features introduced in SQL Server 2005), but you will also have the benefit of using a technically superior product, one that features vastly superior client tools.

NOTE: **Version Requirements Noted**

Any lesson that requires a specific version of SQL Server is clearly noted as such at the start of that lesson.

SQL Server Tools

As just explained, SQL Server is a client/server DBMS, so to use SQL Server you'll need a *client* (an application that you use to interact with SQL Server), giving it commands to be executed.

There are lots of client application options, but when learning SQL Server (and indeed, when writing and testing SQL Server scripts) you are best off using a utility designed for simple script execution. The ideal tool depends on the version of SQL Server being used.

SQL Server 2005

SQL Server 2005 features a sophisticated client tool called Microsoft SQL Server Management Studio. This tool can be used to create and manage databases and tables, control database access and security, run wizards to optimize and fine-tune DBMS performance, and, of course, run SQL statements.

> TIP: **Local or Remote**
>
> Microsoft SQL Server Management Studio can be used to connect to local or remote DBMSs. So long as the DBMS is configured to allow you to connect to it, you can connect to any database anywhere.

There are many ways to use Microsoft SQL Server Management Studio, but here are the basic steps needed to enter and test SQL statements:

▶ The New Query button at the top left of the screen opens a window where SQL statements are entered.

▶ As T-SQL statements are typed, Microsoft SQL Server Management Studio automatically color-codes the statements and text (this is an invaluable troubleshooting tool because it lets you quickly spot typos or missing quotes and so on).

▶ To execute (run) a statement, click the Execute button (the one with the red exclamation point on it). You can also press F5 or Ctrl+E to execute a statement.

- ▶ To verify that a SQL statement is syntactically correct (without executing it), click the Parse button (the one with the blue check mark on it).

- ▶ Microsoft SQL Server Management Studio displays statement results at the bottom of the screen. Results may be displayed in a grid (the default behavior), as plain text, or saved to a file. You can switch between these modes by clicking the appropriate toolbar buttons.

- ▶ In addition to displaying statement results, Microsoft SQL Server Management Studio also displays status messages (the number of rows returned, for example) in a second tab labeled Messages.

- ▶ To obtain help, click the statement you need help with and press F1.

Microsoft SQL Server Management Studio can also be used to execute saved scripts (SQL statements saved in files, such as the sample table-creation and -population scripts mentioned in Appendix B, "The Example Tables"). In fact, all the output examples used in this book are grabs from Microsoft SQL Server Management Studio (using plain-text output).

> **NOTE: Other Tools, Too**
> SQL Server 2005 also installs a whole suite of additional tools and utilities. However, these are beyond the scope of this book.

SQL Server 2000

SQL Server 2000 features an easy-to-use client tool called SQL Query Analyzer. This tool can be used to enter and execute SQL statements. SQL Query Analyzer can be launched directly, or from within another tool called SQL Enterprise Manager (which is used to create and manage databases and tables, control database access and security, and more).

Here are the basic steps needed to enter and test SQL statements using SQL Query Analyzer:

- ▶ The New Query button (the leftmost button on the toolbar) opens a window where SQL statements are entered. You can also press Ctrl+N to open a new query window.

- ▶ As T-SQL statements are typed, SQL Query Analyzer automatically color-codes the statements and text (this is an invaluable troubleshooting tool because it lets you quickly spot typos or missing quotes and so on).

- ▶ To execute (run) a statement, click the Execute button (the one with the green arrow on it). You can also press F5 or Ctrl+E to execute a statement.

- ▶ To verify that a SQL statement is syntactically correct (without executing it), click the Parse button (the one with the blue checkmark on it).

- ▶ SQL Query Analyzer displays statement results at the bottom of the screen. Database retrieval results are displayed in the Grid tab, and messages (the number of rows returned, for example) are displayed in the Messages tab.

Although not as sophisticated as SQL Server 2005's Management Studio, SQL Query Profiler is ideal for experimenting with and learning T-SQL.

Summary

In this lesson, you learned what exactly SQL Server is. You were also introduced to the client utilities (one for each of SQL Server 2005 and SQL Server 2000).

LESSON 3

Working with SQL Server

In this lesson, you'll learn how to connect and log into SQL Server, how to issue SQL Server statements, and how to obtain information about databases and tables.

Making the Connection

Now that you have a SQL Server DBMS and client software to use with it, it would be worthwhile to briefly discuss connecting to the database.

SQL Server, like all client/server DBMSs, requires that you log into the DBMS before being able to issue commands. SQL Server can authenticate users and logins using its own user list, or using the Windows user list (the logins used to start using Windows). As such, depending on how SQL Server is configured, it may log you in automatically using whatever login you used for Windows itself, or it may prompt you for a login name and password.

When you first installed SQL Server, you were probably prompted for an administrative login (often named sa for *system administrator*) and a password. If you are using your own local server and are simply experimenting with SQL Server, using this login is fine. In the real world, however, the administrative login is closely protected because access to it grants full rights to create tables, drop entire databases, change logins and passwords, and more.

To connect to SQL Server, you need the following pieces of information:

- ▶ The hostname (the name of the computer). This is `localhost` or your own computer name if you're connecting to a local SQL Server.

- ▶ A valid username (if Windows authentication is not being used).

- ▶ The user password (if required).

If you're using one of the client applications discussed in the previous lesson, a dialog box will be displayed to prompt you for this information.

> **NOTE: Using Other Clients**
>
> If you are using a client other than the ones mentioned previously, you still need to provide this information in order to connect to SQL Server.

After you are connected, you have access to whatever databases and tables your login name has access to. (Logins, access control, and security are revisited in Lesson 29, "Managing Security.")

Selecting a Database

When you first connect to SQL Server, a default database is opened for you. This will usually be a database named *master* (which as a rule you should never play with). Before you perform any database operations, you need to select the appropriate database. To do this, you use the USE keyword.

> **PLAIN ENGLISH: Keyword**
>
> A reserved word that is part of the T-SQL language. Never name a table or column using a keyword. Appendix E, "T-SQL Reserved Words," lists the SQL Server keywords.

For example, to use the crashcourse database, you would enter the following (in a query window):

Input ▼

```
USE crashcourse;
```

Output ▼

```
Command(s) completed successfully.
```

Analysis ▼

The USE statement does not return any results. Depending on the client used, some form of notification might be displayed (as seen here).

> TIP: **Interactive Database Selection**
>
> In SQL Server Management Studio (or SQL Query Analyzer), you may select a database from the drop-down list in the toolbar to use it. You'll not actually see the USE command being issued (although it is being issued for you), but the database will change and the window title bar will reflect this change.

Remember, you must always USE a database before you can access any data in it.

Learning About Databases and Tables

But what if you don't know the names of the available databases? And for that matter, how do the client applications obtain the list of available databases that are displayed in the drop-down list?

Information about databases, tables, columns, users, privileges, and more, are stored within databases and tables themselves (yes, SQL Server uses SQL Server to store this information). These internal tables are all in the *master* database (which is why you don't want to tamper with it), and they are generally not accessed directly. Instead, SQL Server includes a suite of prewritten stored procedures that can be used to obtain this information (information that SQL Server then extracts from those internal tables).

NOTE: **Stored Procedures**

Stored procedures will be covered in Lesson 23, "Working with Stored Procedures." For now, it will suffice to say that stored procedures are SQL statements that are saved in SQL Server and can be executed as needed.

Look at the following example:

Input ▼

```
sp_databases;
```

Output ▼

```
DATABASE_NAME        DATABASE_SIZE  REMARKS
-----------------    -------------  -------
coldfusion           9096           NULL
crashcourse          3072           NULL
forta                2048           NULL
master               4608           NULL
model                1728           NULL
msdb                 5824           NULL
tempdb               8704           NULL
```

Analysis ▼

sp_databases; returns a list of available databases. Included in this list might be databases used by SQL Server internally (such as master and tempdb in this example). Of course, your own list of databases might not look like those shown above.

To obtain a list of tables within a database, use sp_tables;, as seen here:

Input ▼

```
sp_tables;
```

Analysis ▼

sp_tables; returns a list of available tables in the currently selected database, and not just your tables; it also includes all sorts of system tables and other entries (possibly hundreds of entries).

To obtain a list of tables (just tables, not views, and not system tables and so on), you can use this statement:

Input ▼

```
sp_tables NULL, dbo, crashcourse, "'TABLE'";
```

Output ▼

TABLE_QUALIFIER	TABLE_OWNER	TABLE_NAME	TABLE_TYPE	REMARKS
crashcourse	dbo	customers	TABLE	NULL
crashcourse	dbo	orderitems	TABLE	NULL
crashcourse	dbo	orders	TABLE	NULL
crashcourse	dbo	products	TABLE	NULL
crashcourse	dbo	vendors	TABLE	NULL
crashcourse	dbo	productnotes	TABLE	NULL
crashcourse	dbo	sysdiagrams	TABLE	NULL

Analysis ▼

Here, sp_tables accepts a series of parameters telling it which database to use, as well as what specifically to list ('TABLE' as opposed to 'VIEW' or 'SYSTEM TABLE').

sp_columns can be used to display a table's columns:

Input ▼

```
sp_columns customers;
```

> **NOTE: Shortened for Brevity**
>
> sp_columns returns lots of data. In the output that follows, I have truncated the display because the full output would have been far wider than the pages in this book, likely requiring many lines for each row.

Output ▼

TABLE_QUALIFIER	TABLE_OWNER	TABLE_NAME	COLUMN_NAME	DATA_TYPE	TYPE_NAME
crashcourse	dbo	customers	cust_id	4	int identity
crashcourse	dbo	customers	cust_name	-8	nchar
crashcourse	dbo	customers	cust_address	-8	nchar
crashcourse	dbo	customers	cust_city	-8	nchar
crashcourse	dbo	customers	cust_state	-8	nchar
crashcourse	dbo	customers	cust_zip	-8	nchar
crashcourse	dbo	customers	cust_country	-8	nchar
crashcourse	dbo	customers	cust_contact	-8	nchar
crashcourse	dbo	customers	cust_email	-8	nchar

Analysis ▼

sp_columns requires that a table name be specified (customers in this example), and returns a row for each field, containing the field name, its datatype, whether NULL is allowed, key information, default value, and much more.

NOTE: **What Is Identity?**

Column cust_id is an identity column. Some table columns need unique values (for example, order numbers, employee IDs, or, as in the example just shown, customer IDs). Rather than have to assign unique values manually each time a row is added (and having to keep track of what value was last used), SQL Server can automatically assign the next available number for you each time a row is added to a table. This functionality is known as *identity.* If it is needed, it must be part of the table definition used when the table is created using the CREATE statement. We'll look at CREATE in Lesson 20, "Creating and Manipulating Tables."

Lots of other stored procedures are supported, too, including:

▶ sp_server_info: Used to display extensive server status information

▶ sp_spaceused: Used to display the amount of space used (and unused) by a database

- ▶ `sp_statistics`: Used to display usage statistics pertaining to database tables

- ▶ `sp_helpuser`: Used to display available user accounts

- ▶ `sp_helplogins`: Used to display user logins and what they have rights to

It is worthwhile to note that client applications use these same stored procedures you've seen here. Applications that display interactive lists of databases and tables, that allow for the interactive creation and editing of tables, that facilitate data entry and editing, or that allow for user account and rights management, and more, all accomplish what they do using the same stored procedures that you can execute directly yourself.

Summary

In this lesson, you learned how to connect and log into SQL Server, how to select databases using USE, and how to introspect SQL databases, tables, and internals using stored procedures. Armed with this knowledge, you can now dig into the all-important SELECT statement.

LESSON 4

Retrieving Data

In this lesson, you'll learn how to use the SELECT statement to retrieve one or more columns of data from a table.

The SELECT Statement

As explained in Lesson 1, "Understanding SQL," SQL statements are made up of plain English terms. These terms are called *keywords*, and every SQL statement is made up of one or more keywords. The SQL statement you'll probably use most frequently is the SELECT statement. Its purpose is to retrieve information from one or more tables.

To use SELECT to retrieve table data, at a minimum you must specify two pieces of information: what you want to select and from where you want to select it.

> NOTE: **Make Sure the Right Database Is in Use**
> In order to follow along with the examples, make sure that you are using the right database (the one in which you created and populated the example tables).

Retrieving Individual Columns

We'll start with a simple SQL SELECT statement, as follows:

Input ▼

```
SELECT prod_name
FROM products;
```

Analysis ▼

The previous statement uses the SELECT statement to retrieve a single column called prod_name from the products table. The desired column name is specified right after the SELECT keyword, and the FROM keyword specifies the name of the table from which to retrieve the data. The output. from this statement is shown here:

Output ▼

```
prod_name
--------------
.5 ton anvil
1 ton anvil
2 ton anvil
Detonator
Bird seed
Carrots
Fuses
JetPack 1000
JetPack 2000
Oil can
Safe
Sling
TNT (1 stick)
TNT (5 sticks)
```

> NOTE: **Unsorted Data**
>
> If you tried this query yourself, you might have discovered that the data was displayed in a different order than shown here. If this is the case, don't worry; it is working exactly as it is supposed to. If query results are not explicitly sorted (we'll get to that in the next lesson), data will be returned in no order of any significance. It might be the order in which the data was added to the table, but it might not. As long as your query returned the same number of rows, it is working.

A simple SELECT statement like the one just shown returns all the rows in a table. Data is not filtered (so as to retrieve a subset of the results), nor is it sorted. We'll discuss these topics in the next few lessons.

> **NOTE: Terminating Statements**
>
> Multiple SQL statements must be separated by semicolons (the ; character). SQL Server (like most DBMSs) does not require that a semicolon be specified after single statements. Of course, you can always add a semicolon if you wish. It'll do no harm, even if it isn't needed.

> **NOTE: SQL Statements and Case**
>
> It is important to note that SQL statements are not case sensitive. Therefore, SELECT is the same as select, which is the same as Select. Many SQL developers find that using uppercase for all SQL keywords and lowercase for column and table names makes code easier to read and debug. As a best practice, pick a case convention and use it consistently.

> **TIP: Use of White Space**
>
> All extra white space within a SQL statement is ignored when that statement is processed. SQL statements can be specified on one long line or broken up over many lines. Most SQL developers find that breaking up statements over multiple lines makes them easier to read and debug.

Retrieving Multiple Columns

To retrieve multiple columns from a table, the same SELECT statement is used. The only difference is that multiple column names must be specified after the SELECT keyword, and each column must be separated by a comma.

> **TIP: Take Care with Commas**
>
> When selecting multiple columns, be sure to specify a comma between each column name, but not after the last column name. Doing so will generate an error.

The following SELECT statement retrieves three columns from the products table:

Input ▼

```
SELECT prod_id, prod_name, prod_price
FROM products;
```

Analysis ▼

Just as in the prior example, this statement uses the SELECT statement to retrieve data from the products table. In this example, three column names are specified, each separated by a comma. The output from this statement is as follows:

Output ▼

```
prod_id     prod_name          prod_price
--------    ----------------    ----------
ANV01       .5 ton anvil        5.99
ANV02       1 ton anvil         9.99
ANV03       2 ton anvil         14.99
DTNTR       Detonator           13.00
FB          Bird seed           10.00
FC          Carrots             2.50
FU1         Fuses               3.42
JP1000      JetPack 1000        35.00
JP2000      JetPack 2000        55.00
OL1         Oil can             8.99
SAFE        Safe                50.00
SLING       Sling               4.49
TNT1        TNT (1 stick)       2.50
TNT2        TNT (5 sticks)      10.00
```

> **NOTE: Presentation of Data**
>
> SQL statements typically return raw, unformatted data. Data formatting is a presentation issue, not a retrieval issue. Therefore, presentation (for example, alignment and displaying price values as currency amounts with the currency symbol and commas) is typically specified in the application that displays the data. Actual raw retrieved data (without application-provided formatting) is rarely displayed as is.

Retrieving All Columns

In addition to being able to specify desired columns (one or more, as shown previously), you can use SELECT statements to request all columns without having to list them individually. This is done using the asterisk (*) wildcard character in lieu of actual column names, as follows:

Input ▼

```
SELECT *
FROM products;
```

Analysis ▼

When a wildcard (*) is specified, all the columns in the table are returned. The columns are in the order in which they appear in the table definition. However, this cannot be relied on because changes to table schemas (adding and removing columns, for example) could cause ordering changes.

CAUTION: **Using Wildcards**

As a rule, you are better off not using the * wildcard unless you really do need every column in the table. Even though use of wildcards might save you the time and effort needed to list the desired columns explicitly, retrieving unnecessary columns usually slows down the performance of your retrieval and your application.

TIP: **Retrieving Unknown Columns**

There is one big advantage to using wildcards. Because you do not explicitly specify column names (because the asterisk retrieves every column), it is possible to retrieve columns whose names are unknown.

Retrieving Distinct Rows

As you have seen, SELECT returns all matched rows. But what if you did
not want every occurrence of every value? For example, suppose you want
the vendor ID of all vendors with products in your products table:

Input ▼

```
SELECT vend_id
FROM products;
```

Output ▼

```
vend_id
-----------
1001
1001
1001
1003
1003
1003
1002
1005
1005
1002
1003
1003
1003
1003
```

The SELECT statement returned 14 rows (even though only four vendors
are in that list) because there are 14 products listed in the products table.
So how could you retrieve a list of distinct values?

The solution is to use the DISTINCT keyword, which, as its name implies,
instructs SQL Server to only return distinct values:

Input ▼

```
SELECT DISTINCT vend_id
FROM products;
```

Analysis ▼

SELECT DISTINCT vend_id tells SQL Server to only return distinct (unique) vend_id rows, and therefore only four rows are returned, as shown in the following output. If used, the DISTINCT keyword must be placed directly in front of the column names.

Output ▼

```
vend_id
----------
1001
1002
1003
1005
```

> CAUTION: **Can't Be Partially** DISTINCT
>
> The DISTINCT keyword applies to all columns, not just the one it precedes. If you were to specify SELECT DISTINCT vend_id, prod_price, all rows would be retrieved unless *both* of the specified columns were distinct.

Limiting Results

SELECT statements return all matched rows, possibly every row in the specified table. To return just the first row or rows, use the TOP keyword. Here is an example:

Input ▼

```
SELECT TOP(5) prod_name
FROM products;
```

Analysis ▼

The previous statement uses the SELECT statement to retrieve a single column. TOP(5) instructs SQL Server to return no more than five rows. The output from this statement is shown next:

Output ▼

```
prod_name
- - - - - - - - - - - -
.5 ton anvil
1 ton anvil
2 ton anvil
Detonator
Bird seed
```

> **NOTE: SQL Server 6.5 or Later**
>
> Support for TOP was introduced into T-SQL in SQL Server 6.5. If you are using an earlier version of SQL Server, use SET ROWCOUNT instead, as shown here:
>
> SET ROWCOUNT 5;
> SELECTprod_name
> FROM products;
>
> SET ROWCOUNT is still supported in newer versions of SQL Server, but generally use of TOP is preferred.

You can also use TOP to get a percentage of rows by adding the keyword PERCENT. Here is an example:

Input ▼

```
SELECT TOP(25) PERCENT prod_name
FROM products;
```

Analysis ▼

TOP(25) PERCENT instructs SQL Server to return the first 25% of rows in the products table. The output from this statement is shown here:

Output ▼

```
prod_name
- - - - - - - - - - - -
.5 ton anvil
1 ton anvil
2 ton anvil
Detonator
```

> **NOTE: When There Aren't Enough Rows**
> The number of rows to retrieve as specified in TOP is the *maximum* number to retrieve. If there aren't enough rows (for example, you specified TOP(20), but there were only 14 rows), SQL Server returns as many as it can.

New to SQL Server 2005 is support for retrieving a random sampling of rows by using the TABLESAMPLE keyword. Here are a couple of examples:

Input ▼

```
SELECT * FROM products
TABLESAMPLE (3 ROWS);
```

Analysis ▼

TABLESAMPLE allows you to specify how many rows to retrieve, and this example would retrieve 3 random rows.

Input ▼

```
SELECT * FROM products
TABLESAMPLE (50 PERCENT);
```

Analysis ▼

Here TABLESAMPLE is used to specify a percentage of table contents, in this example 50 PERCENT.

It is worth noting that you may not get the exact number of rows that you'd expect. Sampling occurs by table page (the internal mechanism used by SQL Server to actually store data), and the number of rows in a page can vary.

Using Fully Qualified Table Names

The SQL examples used thus far have referred to columns by just the column names. It is also possible to refer to columns using fully qualified names (using both the table and column names). Look at this example:

Input ▼

```
SELECT products.prod_name
FROM products;
```

This SQL statement is functionally identical to the very first one used in this lesson, but here a fully qualified column name is specified.

Table names, too, may be fully qualified, as shown here:

Input ▼

```
SELECT products.prod_name
FROM crashcourse.dbo.products;
```

Once again, this statement is functionally identical to the one just used (assuming, of course, that the products table is indeed in the crashcourse database). But notice the extra dbo in the table name. A fully qualified table name is made up of a database name, the table owner name, and the table name. The default owner will always be dbo (as in *database owner*), and therefore crashcourse.dbo.products is the fully qualified name for table products in the crashcourse database.

In certain situations fully qualified names are required, as you will see in later lessons. For now, it is worth noting this syntax so you'll know what it is if you run across it.

Summary

In this lesson, you learned how to use the SQL SELECT statement to retrieve a single table column, multiple table columns, and all table columns. Next you'll learn how to sort the retrieved data.

LESSON 5

Sorting Retrieved Data

In this lesson, you will learn how to use the SELECT statement's ORDER BY clause to sort retrieved data as needed.

Sorting Data

As you learned in the last lesson, the following SQL statement returns a single column from a database table. But look at the output. The data appears to be displayed in no particular order at all.

Input ▼

```
SELECT prod_name
FROM products;
```

Output ▼

```
prod_name
-------------
.5 ton anvil
1 ton anvil
2 ton anvil
Detonator
Bird seed
Carrots
Fuses
JetPack 1000
JetPack 2000
Oil can
Safe
Sling
TNT (1 stick)
TNT (5 sticks)
```

Actually, the retrieved data is not displayed in a mere random order. If unsorted, data is typically displayed in the order in which it appears in the underlying tables. This could be the order in which the data was added to the tables initially. However, if data was subsequently updated or deleted, the order is affected by how SQL Server reuses reclaimed storage space. The end result is that you cannot (and should not) rely on the sort order if you do not explicitly control it. Relational database design theory states that the sequence of retrieved data cannot be assumed to have significance if ordering is not explicitly specified.

> PLAIN ENGLISH: **Clause**
>
> SQL statements are made up of clauses, some required and some optional. A clause usually consists of a keyword and supplied data. An example of this is the SELECT statement's FROM clause, which you saw in the last lesson.

To explicitly sort data retrieved using a SELECT statement, you use the ORDER BY clause. ORDER BY takes the name of one or more columns by which to sort the output. Look at the following example:

Input ▼

```
SELECT prod_name
FROM products
ORDER BY prod_name;
```

Analysis ▼

This statement is identical to the earlier statement, except it also specifies an ORDER BY clause instructing SQL Server to sort the data alphabetically by the prod_name column. The results are as follows:

Output ▼

```
prod_name
--------------
.5 ton anvil
1 ton anvil
2 ton anvil
```

```
Bird seed
Carrots
Detonator
Fuses
JetPack 1000
JetPack 2000
Oil can
Safe
Sling
TNT (1 stick)
TNT (5 sticks)
```

> TIP: **Sorting by Nonselected Columns**
> More often than not, the columns used in an ORDER BY clause are ones that were selected for display. However, this is actually not required, and it is perfectly legal to sort data by a column that is not retrieved.

Sorting by Multiple Columns

It is often necessary to sort data by more than one column. For example, if you are displaying an employee list, you might want to display it sorted by last name and first name (first sort by last name, and then within each last name sort by first name). This would be useful if multiple employees have the same last name.

To sort by multiple columns, simply specify the column names separated by commas (just as you do when you are selecting multiple columns).

The following code retrieves three columns and sorts the results by two of them, first by price and then by name.

Input ▼

```
SELECT prod_id, prod_price, prod_name
FROM products
ORDER BY prod_price, prod_name;
```

Output ▼

prod_id	prod_price	prod_name
FC	2.50	Carrots
TNT1	2.50	TNT (1 stick)
FU1	3.42	Fuses
SLING	4.49	Sling
ANV01	5.99	.5 ton anvil
OL1	8.99	Oil can
ANV02	9.99	1 ton anvil
FB	10.00	Bird seed
TNT2	10.00	TNT (5 sticks)
DTNTR	13.00	Detonator
ANV03	14.99	2 ton anvil
JP1000	35.00	JetPack 1000
SAFE	50.00	Safe
JP2000	55.00	JetPack 2000

It is important to understand that when you are sorting by multiple columns, the sort sequence is exactly as specified. In other words, using the output in the previous example, the products are sorted by the prod_name column only when multiple rows have the same prod_price value. If all the values in the prod_price column had been unique, no data would have been sorted by prod_name.

Specifying Sort Direction

Data sorting is not limited to ascending sort orders (from A to Z). Although this is the default sort order, the ORDER BY clause can also be used to sort in descending order (from Z to A). To sort by descending order, you must specify the keyword DESC.

The following example sorts the products by price in descending order (most expensive first):

Input ▼

```
SELECT prod_id, prod_price, prod_name
FROM products
ORDER BY prod_price DESC;
```

Output ▼

prod_id	prod_price	prod_name
JP2000	55.00	JetPack 2000
SAFE	50.00	Safe
JP1000	35.00	JetPack 1000
ANV03	14.99	2 ton anvil
DTNTR	13.00	Detonator
TNT2	10.00	TNT (5 sticks)
FB	10.00	Bird seed
ANV02	9.99	1 ton anvil
OL1	8.99	Oil can
ANV01	5.99	.5 ton anvil
SLING	4.49	Sling
FU1	3.42	Fuses
FC	2.50	Carrots
TNT1	2.50	TNT (1 stick)

But what if you were to sort by multiple columns, how would that impact sort direction? The following example sorts the products in descending order (most expensive first), plus provides the product name:

Input ▼

```
SELECT prod_id, prod_price, prod_name
FROM products
ORDER BY prod_price DESC, prod_name;
```

Output ▼

prod_id	prod_price	prod_name
JP2000	55.00	JetPack 2000
SAFE	50.00	Safe
JP1000	35.00	JetPack 1000
ANV03	14.99	2 ton anvil
DTNTR	13.00	Detonator
FB	10.00	Bird seed
TNT2	10.00	TNT (5 sticks)
ANV02	9.99	1 ton anvil
OL1	8.99	Oil can
ANV01	5.99	.5 ton anvil
SLING	4.49	Sling
FU1	3.42	Fuses
FC	2.50	Carrots
TNT1	2.50	TNT (1 stick)

Analysis ▼

The DESC keyword only applies to the column name that directly precedes it. In the previous example, DESC was specified for the prod_price column, but not for the prod_name column. Therefore, the prod_price column is sorted in descending order, but the prod_name column (within each price) is still sorted in standard ascending order.

TIP: **Sorting Descending on Multiple Columns**

If you want to sort in descending order on multiple columns, be sure each column has its own DESC keyword.

The opposite of DESC is ASC (for *ascending*), which may be specified to sort in ascending order. In practice, however, ASC is not generally used because ascending order is the default sequence (and is assumed if neither ASC nor DESC is specified).

TIP: **Case Sensitivity and Sort Orders**

When you are sorting textual data, is A the same as a? And does a come before B or after Z? These are not theoretical questions, and the answers depend on how the database is set up.

In *dictionary* sort order, A is treated the same as a, and that is the default behavior in SQL Server (and indeed most DBMSs). However, administrators can change this behavior if needed. (If your database contains lots of foreign language characters, this might become necessary.)

The key here is that, if you do need an alternate sort order, you cannot accomplish it with a simple ORDER BY clause. You must contact your database administrator.

Using a combination of ORDER BY and TOP, it is possible to find the highest or lowest value in a column. The following example demonstrates how to find the value of the most expensive item:

Input ▼

```
SELECT TOP(1) prod_price
FROM products
ORDER BY prod_price DESC;
```

Output ▼

```
prod_price
--------------------
55.00
```

Analysis ▼

prod_price DESC ensures that rows are retrieved from most to least expensive, and TOP(1) tells SQL Server to just return one row.

> CAUTION: **Position of the** ORDER BY **Clause**
>
> When specifying an ORDER BY clause, be sure that it is after the FROM clause. Using clauses out of order will generate an error message.

Summary

In this lesson, you learned how to sort retrieved data using the SELECT statement's ORDER BY clause. This clause, which must be the last in the SELECT statement, can be used to sort data on one or more columns, as needed.

LESSON 6

Filtering Data

In this lesson, you will learn how to use the SELECT statement's WHERE clause to specify search conditions.

Using the WHERE Clause

Database tables usually contain large amounts of data, and you seldom need to retrieve all the rows in a table. More often than not, you'll want to extract a subset of the table's data as needed for specific operations or reports. Retrieving just the data you want involves specifying *search criteria*, also known as a *filter condition*.

Within a SELECT statement, you filter data by specifying search criteria in the WHERE clause. The WHERE clause is specified right after the table name (using the FROM clause) as follows:

Input ▼

```
SELECT prod_name, prod_price
FROM products
WHERE prod_price = 2.50;
```

Analysis ▼

This statement retrieves two columns from the products table, but instead of returning all rows, it returns only rows with a prod_price value of 2.50, as shown here:

Output ▼

```
prod_name       prod_price
--------------  ----------
Carrots         2.50
TNT (1 stick)   2.50
```

This example uses a simple equality test: It checks to see if a column has a specified value, and it filters the data accordingly. However, T-SQL enables you to do more than just test for equality.

TIP: **SQL Versus Application Filtering**

Data can also be filtered at the application level. To do this, the SQL SELECT statement retrieves more data than is actually required for the client application, and the client code loops through the returned data to extract just the needed rows.

As a rule, this practice is strongly discouraged. DBMSs are optimized to perform filtering quickly and efficiently. Making the client application (or development language) do the database's job dramatically impacts application performance and creates applications that cannot scale properly. In addition, if data is filtered at the client, the server has to send unneeded data across the network connections, resulting in a waste of network bandwidth resources.

CAUTION: WHERE **Clause Position**

When using both ORDER BY and WHERE clauses, make sure ORDER BY comes after WHERE; otherwise, an error will be generated. (See Lesson 5, "Sorting Retrieved Data," for more information on using ORDER BY.)

The WHERE Clause Operators

The first WHERE clause we looked at tests for equality, determining if a column contains a specific value. T-SQL supports a whole range of comparison operators, some of which are listed in Table 6.1.

TABLE 6.1 WHERE Clause Operators

Operator	Description
=	Equality
<>	Nonequality
!=	Nonequality
<	Less than
<=	Less than or equal to
!<	Not less than
>	Greater than
>=	Greater than or equal to
!>	Not greater than
BETWEEN	Between two specified values
IS NULL	Is a NULL value

Checking Against a Single Value

You have already seen an example of testing for equality. Here's one more:

Input ▼

```
SELECT prod_name, prod_price
FROM products
WHERE prod_name = 'fuses';
```

Output ▼

```
prod_name    prod_price
----------   ----------
Fuses        3.42
```

Analysis ▼

Checking for WHERE prod_name = 'fuses' returned a single row with a value of Fuses. By default, T-SQL is not case sensitive when performing matches, and therefore fuses and Fuses matched.

Now we'll look at a few examples to demonstrate the use of other operators.

This first example lists all products that cost less than 10:

Input ▼

```
SELECT prod_name, prod_price
FROM products
WHERE prod_price < 10;
```

Output ▼

```
prod_name       prod_price
--------------  ----------
.5 ton anvil    5.99
1 ton anvil     9.99
Carrots         2.50
Fuses           3.42
Oil can         8.99
Sling           4.49
TNT (1 stick)   2.50
```

This next statement retrieves all products costing 10 or less (resulting in two additional matches):

Input ▼

```
SELECT prod_name, prod_price
FROM products
WHERE prod_price <= 10;
```

Output ▼

```
prod_name        prod_price
--------------   ----------
.5 ton anvil     5.99
1 ton anvil      9.99
Bird seed        10.00
Carrots          2.50
Fuses            3.42
Oil can          8.99
Sling            4.49
TNT (1 stick)    2.50
TNT (5 sticks)   10.00
```

Checking for Nonmatches

This example lists all products not made by vendor 1003:

Input ▼

```
SELECT vend_id, prod_name
FROM products
WHERE vend_id <> 1003;
```

Output ▼

```
vend_id      prod_name
----------   ------------
1001         .5 ton anvil
1001         1 ton anvil
1001         2 ton anvil
1002         Fuses
1005         JetPack 1000
1005         JetPack 2000
1002         Oil can
```

> TIP: **When to Use Quotes**
>
> If you look closely at the conditions used in the examples' WHERE
> clauses, you will notice that some values are enclosed within single
> quotes (such as 'fuses', used previously) and others are not. The
> single quotes are used to delimit strings. If you are comparing a
> value against a column that is a string *datatype*, the delimiting
> quotes are required. Quotes are not used to delimit values used
> with numeric columns.

The following is the same example, except this one uses the != operator
instead of <>:

Input ▼

```
SELECT vend_id, prod_name
FROM products
WHERE vend_id != 1003;
```

Checking for a Range of Values

To check for a range of values, you can use the BETWEEN operator. Its syntax is a little different from other WHERE clause operators because it requires two values: the beginning and end of the range. The BETWEEN operator can be used, for example, to check for all products that cost between 5 and 10 or for all dates that fall between specified start and end dates.

The following example demonstrates the use of the BETWEEN operator by retrieving all products with a price between 5 and 10:

Input ▼

```
SELECT prod_name, prod_price
FROM products
WHERE prod_price BETWEEN 5 AND 10;
```

Output ▼

```
prod_name          prod_price
---------------    ----------
.5 ton anvil       5.99
1 ton anvil        9.99
Bird seed          10.00
Oil can            8.99
TNT (5 sticks)     10.00
```

Analysis ▼

As shown in this example, when BETWEEN is used, two values must be specified, the low end and high end of the desired range. The two values must also be separated by the AND keyword. BETWEEN matches all the values in the range, including the specified range start and end values.

Checking for No Value

When a table is created, the table designer can specify whether individual columns can contain no value. When a column contains no value, it is said to contain a NULL value.

> PLAIN ENGLISH: NULL
>
> *No value*, as opposed to a field containing 0, an empty string, or just spaces.

The SELECT statement has a special WHERE clause that can be used to check for columns with NULL values, the IS NULL clause. The syntax looks like this:

Input ▼

```
SELECT prod_name
FROM products
WHERE prod_price IS NULL;
```

This statement returns a list of all products that have no price (an empty prod_price field, not a price of 0), and because there are none, no data is returned. The customers table, however, does contain columns with NULL values; the cust_email column contains NULL if a customer has no email address on file:

Input ▼

```
SELECT cust_id
FROM customers
WHERE cust_email IS NULL;
```

Output ▼

```
cust_id
-----------
10002
10005
```

CAUTION: NULL **and Nonmatches**
You might expect that when you filter to select all rows that do not have a particular value, rows with a NULL will be returned. But they will not. Because of the special meaning of *unknown*, the database does not know whether these rows match, so they are not returned when filtering for matches or when filtering for nonmatches.

When filtering data, make sure to verify that the rows with a NULL in the filtered column are really present in the returned data.

Summary

In this lesson, you learned how to filter returned data using the SELECT statement's WHERE clause. You learned how to test for equality, nonequality, greater than and less than, value ranges, and NULL values.

LESSON 7

Advanced Data Filtering

In this lesson, you'll learn how to combine WHERE clauses to create powerful and sophisticated search conditions. You'll also learn how to use the NOT and IN operators.

Combining WHERE Clauses

All the WHERE clauses introduced in Lesson 6, "Filtering Data," filter data using a single criteria. For a greater degree of filter control, T-SQL allows you to specify multiple WHERE clauses. These clauses may be used in two ways: as AND clauses or as OR clauses.

> PLAIN ENGLISH: **Operator**
> A special keyword used to join or change clauses within a WHERE clause. Also known as a *logical operator*.

Using the AND Operator

To filter by more than one column, you use the AND operator to append conditions to your WHERE clause. The following code demonstrates this:

Input ▼

```
SELECT prod_id, prod_price, prod_name
FROM products
WHERE vend_id = 1003 AND prod_price <= 10;
```

Analysis ▼

The preceding SQL statement retrieves the product name and price for all products made by vendor 1003 as long as the price is 10 or less. The WHERE clause in this SELECT statement is made up of two conditions, and the keyword AND is used to join them. AND instructs the SQL Server to return only rows that meet all the conditions specified. If a product is made by vendor 1003 but it costs more than 10, it is not retrieved. Similarly, products that cost less than 10 that are made by a vendor other than the one specified are not retrieved. The output generated by this SQL statement is as follows:

Output ▼

```
prod_id    prod_price              prod_name
---------  ----------------------  ---------------
FB         10.00                   Bird seed
FC         2.50                    Carrots
SLING      4.49                    Sling
TNT1       2.50                    TNT (1 stick)
TNT2       10.00                   TNT (5 sticks)
```

PLAIN ENGLISH: AND

A keyword used in a WHERE clause to specify that only rows matching all the specified conditions should be retrieved.

The current example contains a single AND clause and is thus made up of two filter conditions. Additional filter conditions can be used as well, each seperated by an AND keyword.

Using the OR Operator

As just seen, AND requires that both conditions be met for a row to be retrieved. The OR operator instructs SQL Server to retrieve rows that match *either* condition, so if one matches and one does not, the row would still be retrieved.

Look at the following SELECT statement:

Input ▼

```
SELECT prod_name, prod_price
FROM products
WHERE vend_id = 1002 OR vend_id = 1003;
```

Analysis ▼

This SQL statement retrieves the product name and price for any products made by either of the two specified vendors. The OR operator tells the DBMS to match either condition, not necessarily both. If an AND operator would have been used here, no data would be returned. (It would have created a WHERE clause that could never be matched.) The output generated by this SQL statement is as follows:

Output ▼

```
prod_name          prod_price
---------------    ----------
Detonator          13.00
Bird seed          10.00
Carrots            2.50
Fuses              3.42
Oil can            8.99
Safe               50.00
Sling              4.49
TNT (1 stick)      2.50
TNT (5 sticks)     10.00
```

> PLAIN ENGLISH: OR
>
> A keyword used in a WHERE clause to specify that any rows matching either of the specified conditions should be retrieved.

Understanding Order of Evaluation

WHERE clauses can contain any number of AND and OR operators. Combining the two enables you to perform sophisticated and complex filtering.

However, combining AND and OR operators presents an interesting problem. To demonstrate this, let's look at an example. Suppose you need a list of all products costing 10 or more made by vendors 1002 and 1003. The following SELECT statement uses a combination of AND and OR operators to build a WHERE clause:

Input ▼

```
SELECT prod_name, prod_price
FROM products
WHERE vend_id = 1002 OR vend_id = 1003 AND prod_price >= 10;
```

Output ▼

```
prod_name          prod_price
---------------    ----------
Detonator          13.00
Bird seed          10.00
Fuses              3.42
Oil can            8.99
Safe               50.00
TNT (5 sticks)     10.00
```

Analysis ▼

Look at the listed results. Two of the rows returned have prices less than 10; so, obviously, the rows were not filtered as intended. Why did this happen? The answer is the order of evaluation. T-SQL (like most languages) processes AND operators before OR operators. When SQL Server sees the preceding WHERE clause, it reads *products made by vendor 1002 regardless of price, and any products costing 10 or more made by vendor 1003*. In other words, because AND ranks higher in the order of evaluation, the wrong operators were joined together.

The solution to this problem is to use parentheses to explicitly group related operators. Take a look at the following SELECT statement and output:

Input ▼

```
SELECT prod_name, prod_price
FROM products
WHERE (vend_id = 1002 OR vend_id = 1003) AND prod_price >= 10;
```

Output ▼

```
prod_name        prod_price
---------------- ----------
Detonator        13.00
Bird seed        10.00
Safe             50.00
TNT (5 sticks)   10.00
```

Analysis ▼

The only difference between this SELECT statement and the earlier one is that, in this statement, the first two WHERE clause conditions are enclosed within parentheses. Because parentheses have a higher order of evaluation than either AND or OR operators, SQL Server first filters the OR condition within those parentheses. The SQL statement then becomes *any products made by either vendor 1002 or vendor 1003 costing 10 or greater*, which is exactly what you want.

TIP: **Using Parentheses in** WHERE **Clauses**
Whenever you write WHERE clauses that use both AND and OR operators, use parentheses to explicitly group the operators. Don't ever rely on the default evaluation order, even if it is exactly what you want. There is no downside to using parentheses, and you are always better off eliminating any ambiguity.

Using the IN Operator

Parentheses have another very different use in WHERE clauses. The IN operator is used to specify a range of conditions, any of which can be matched. IN takes a comma-delimited list of valid values, all enclosed within parentheses. The following example demonstrates this:

Input ▼

```
SELECT prod_name, prod_price
FROM products
WHERE vend_id IN (1002,1003)
ORDER BY prod_name;
```

Output ▼

```
prod_name        prod_price
---------------- ----------
Bird seed        10.00
Carrots          2.50
Detonator        13.00
Fuses            3.42
Oil can          8.99
Safe             50.00
Sling            4.49
TNT (1 stick)    2.50
TNT (5 sticks)   10.00
```

Analysis ▼

The SELECT statement retrieves all products made by vendor 1002 and vendor 1003. The IN operator is followed by a comma-delimited list of valid values, and the entire list must be enclosed within parentheses.

If you are thinking that the IN operator accomplishes the same goal as OR, you are right. The following SQL statement accomplishes the exact same thing as the previous example:

Input ▼

```
SELECT prod_name, prod_price
FROM products
WHERE vend_id  = 1002 OR vend_id = 1003
ORDER BY prod_name;
```

Output ▼

```
prod_name        prod_price
---------------- ----------
Bird seed        10.00
Carrots          2.50
Detonator        13.00
Fuses            3.42
Oil can          8.99
Safe             50.00
Sling            4.49
TNT (1 stick)    2.50
TNT (5 sticks)   10.00
```

Why use the IN operator? Here are the advantages:

▶ When you are working with long lists of valid options, the IN operator syntax is far cleaner and easier to read.

▶ The order of evaluation is easier to manage when IN is used (because fewer operators are used).

▶ IN operators almost always execute more quickly than lists of OR operators.

▶ The biggest advantage of IN is that the IN operator can contain another SELECT statement, enabling you to build highly dynamic WHERE clauses. You'll look at this in detail in Lesson 13, "Working with Subqueries."

> **PLAIN ENGLISH: IN**
>
> A keyword used in a WHERE clause to specify a list of values to be matched using an OR comparison.

Using the NOT Operator

The WHERE clause's NOT operator has one function and one function only: NOT negates whatever condition comes next.

> **PLAIN ENGLISH: NOT**
>
> A keyword used in a WHERE clause to negate a condition.

The following example demonstrates the use of NOT. To list the products made by all vendors except vendors 1002 and 1003, you can use the following:

Input ▼

```
SELECT prod_name, prod_price
FROM products
WHERE vend_id NOT IN (1002,1003)
ORDER BY prod_name;
```

Output ▼

```
prod_name        prod_price
---------------  ----------
.5 ton anvil     5.99
1 ton anvil      9.99
2 ton anvil      14.99
JetPack 1000     35.00
JetPack 2000     55.00
```

Analysis ▼

The NOT here negates the condition that follows it; so instead of matching vend_id to 1002 or 1003, SQL Server matches vend_id to anything that is not 1002 or 1003.

So why use NOT? Well, for simple WHERE clauses, there really is no advantage to using NOT. NOT is useful in more complex clauses. For example, using NOT in conjunction with an IN operator makes it simple to find all rows that do not match a list of criteria.

Summary

This lesson picked up where the last lesson left off and taught you how to combine WHERE clauses with the AND and OR operators. You also learned how to explicitly manage the order of evaluation and how to use the IN and NOT operators.

LESSON 8

Using Wildcard Filtering

In this lesson, you'll learn what wildcards are, how they are used, and how to perform wildcard searches using the LIKE operator for sophisticated filtering of retrieved data.

Using the LIKE Operator

All the previous operators we studied filter against known values. Be it matching one or more values, testing for greater-than or less-than known values, or checking a range of values, the common denominator is that the values used in the filtering are known. But filtering data that way does not always work. For example, how could you search for all products that contain the text *anvil* within the product name? That cannot be done with simple comparison operators; that's a job for wildcard searching. Using wildcards, you can create search patterns that can be compared against your data. In this example, if you want to find all products that contain the words *anvil*, you could construct a wildcard search pattern enabling you to find that *anvil* text anywhere within a product name.

> PLAIN ENGLISH: **Wildcards**
> Special characters used to match parts of a value.

> PLAIN ENGLISH: **Search pattern**
> A search condition made up of literal text, wildcard characters, or any combination of the two.

The wildcards themselves are actually characters that have special meanings within SQL WHERE clauses, and SQL supports several wildcard types.

To use wildcards in search clauses, you must use the LIKE operator. LIKE instructs SQL Server that the following search pattern is to be compared using a wildcard match rather than a straight equality match.

> **NOTE: Predicates**
>
> When is an operator not an operator? When it is a *predicate*. Technically, LIKE is a predicate, not an operator. The end result is the same; just be aware of this term in case you run across it in the SQL Server documentation.

The Percent Sign (%) Wildcard

The most frequently used wildcard is the percent sign (%). Within a search string, % means *match any number of occurrences of any character*. For example, to find all products that start with the word jet, you can issue the following SELECT statement:

Input ▼

```
SELECT prod_id, prod_name
FROM products
WHERE prod_name LIKE 'jet%';
```

Output ▼

```
prod_id     prod_name
---------- ----------------
JP1000      JetPack 1000
JP2000      JetPack 2000
```

Analysis ▼

This example uses a search pattern of 'jet%'. When this clause is evaluated, any value that starts with jet is retrieved. The % tells SQL Server to accept any characters after the word jet, regardless of how many characters there are.

> NOTE: **Case sensitivity**
> Depending on how SQL Server is configured, searches might be case sensitive, in which case `'jet%'` would not match `JetPack 1000`. But the default behavior on most SQL Server installations is case-insensitive.

Wildcards can be used anywhere within the search pattern, and multiple wildcards can be used as well. The following example uses two wildcards, one at either end of the pattern:

Input ▼

```
SELECT prod_id, prod_name
FROM products
WHERE prod_name LIKE '%anvil%';
```

Output ▼

```
prod_id     prod_name
----------  --------------
ANV01       .5 ton anvil
ANV02       1 ton anvil
ANV03       2 ton anvil
```

Analysis ▼

The search pattern `'%anvil%'` means *match any value that contains the text* anvil *anywhere within it, regardless of any characters before or after that text.*

Wildcards can also be used in the middle of a search pattern, although that is rarely useful. The following example finds all products that begin with an s and end with an e:

Input ▼

```
SELECT prod_name
FROM products
WHERE prod_name LIKE 's%e';
```

It is important to note that, in addition to matching one or more characters, % also matches zero characters. % represents zero, one, or more characters at the specified location in the search pattern.

NOTE: **Watch for Trailing Spaces**

Trailing spaces can interfere with wildcard matching. For example, if any of the instances of *anvil* had been saved with one or more spaces after the word, the clause WHERE prod_name LIKE '%anvil' would not have matched them because of the additional characters after the final 1. One simple solution to this problem is to always append a final % to the search pattern. A better solution is to trim the spaces using functions, as discussed in Lesson 10, "Using Data Manipulation Functions."

CAUTION: **Watch for NULL**

Although it may seem that the % wildcard matches anything, there is one exception, NULL. Not even the clause WHERE prod_name LIKE '%' will match a row with the value NULL as the product name.

The Underscore (_) Wildcard

Another useful wildcard is the underscore (_). The underscore is used just like %, but instead of matching multiple characters, the underscore matches just a single character.

Take a look at this example:

Input ▼

```
SELECT prod_id, prod_name
FROM products
WHERE prod_name LIKE '_ ton anvil%';
```

Output ▼

```
prod_id     prod_name
---------   -------------
ANV02       1 ton anvil
ANV03       2 ton anvil
```

Analysis ▼

The search pattern used in this WHERE clause specifies a wildcard followed by literal text. The results shown are the only rows that match the search pattern: The underscore matches 1 in the first row and 2 in the second row. The .5 ton anvil product did not match because the search pattern matched a single character, not two. By contrast, the following SELECT statement uses the % wildcard and returns three matching products:

Input ▼

```
SELECT prod_id, prod_name
FROM products
WHERE prod_name LIKE '% ton anvil%';
```

Output ▼

```
prod_id    prod_name
---------- --------------
ANV01      .5 ton anvil
ANV02      1 ton anvil
ANV03      2 ton anvil
```

Unlike %, which can match zero characters, _ always matches one character, no more and no less.

The Brackets ([ ]) Wildcard

The brackets ([ ]) wildcard is used to specify a set of characters, any one of which must match a character in the specified position (the location of the wildcard).

For example, to find all contacts whose names begin with the letter *J* or the letter *M*, you can do the following:

Input ▼

```
SELECT cust_contact
FROM customers
WHERE cust_contact LIKE '[EJ]%'
ORDER BY cust_contact;
```

Output ▼

```
cust_contact
---------------
E Fudd
Jerry Mouse
Jim Jones
```

Analysis ▼

The WHERE clause in this statement is '[EJ]%'. This search pattern uses two different wildcards. The [EJ] matches any contact name that begins with either of the letters within the brackets, and it also matches only a single character. Therefore, any names longer than one character do not match. The % wildcard after the [EJ] matches any number of characters after the first character, thus returning the desired results.

This wildcard can be negated by prefixing the characters with ^ (the carat character). For example, the following matches any contact name that does not begin with the letter *E* or the letter *J* (the opposite of the previous example):

Input ▼

```
SELECT cust_contact
FROM customers
WHERE cust_contact LIKE '[^EJ]%'
ORDER BY cust_contact;
```

Of course, you can accomplish the same result using the NOT operator. The only advantage of ^ is that it can simplify the syntax if you are using multiple WHERE clauses:

Input ▼

```
SELECT cust_contact
FROM Customers
WHERE NOT cust_contact LIKE '[EJ]%'
ORDER BY cust_contact;
```

Tips for Using Wildcards

As you can see, T-SQL's wildcards are extremely powerful. But that power comes with a price: Wildcard searches typically take far longer to process than any other search types discussed previously. Here are some tips to keep in mind when using wildcards:

- ▶ Don't overuse wildcards. If another search operator will do, use it instead.

- ▶ When you do use wildcards, try not to use them at the beginning of the search pattern unless absolutely necessary. Search patterns that begin with wildcards are the slowest to process.

- ▶ Pay careful attention to the placement of the wildcard symbols. If they are misplaced, you might not return the data you intended.

Having said that, wildcards are an important and useful search tool, and one that you will use frequently.

Summary

In this lesson, you learned what wildcards are and how to use SQL wildcards within your WHERE clauses. You also learned that wildcards should be used carefully and never overused.

Creating Calculated Fields

In this lesson, you will learn what calculated fields are, how to create them, and how to use aliases to refer to them from within your application.

Understanding Calculated Fields

Data stored within a database's tables is often not available in the exact format needed by your applications. Here are some examples:

- ▶ You need to display a field containing the name of a company along with the company's location, but that information is stored in separated table columns.

- ▶ City, state, and ZIP Code are stored in separate columns (as they should be), but your mailing label printing program needs them retrieved as one correctly formatted field.

- ▶ Column data is in mixed upper- and lowercase, and your report needs all data presented in uppercase.

- ▶ An order items table stores item price and quantity but not the expanded price (price multiplied by quantity) of each item. To print invoices, you need that expanded price.

- ▶ You need total, averages, or other calculations based on table data.

In each of these examples, the data stored in the table is not exactly what your application needs. Rather than retrieve the data as it is and then reformat it within your client application or report, what you really want is to retrieve converted, calculated, or reformatted data directly from the database.

This is where calculated fields come in. Unlike all the columns we retrieved in the lessons thus far, calculated fields don't actually exist in database tables. Rather, a calculated field is created on the fly within a SQL SELECT statement.

> **PLAIN ENGLISH: Field**
> Essentially means the same thing as *column* and often is used interchangeably, although database columns are typically called *columns* and the term *fields* is normally used in conjunction with calculated fields.

It is important to note that only the database knows which columns in a SELECT statement are actual table columns and which are calculated fields. From the perspective of a client (for example, your application), a calculated field's data is returned in the same way as data from any other column.

> **TIP: Client Versus Server Formatting**
> Many of the conversions and reformatting that can be performed within SQL statements can also be performed directly in your client application. However, as a rule, it is far quicker to perform these operations on the database server than it is to perform them within the client because Database Management Systems (DBMSs) are built to perform this type of processing quickly and efficiently.

Concatenating Fields

To demonstrate working with calculated fields, let's start with a simple example, creating a title made up of two columns.

The vendors table contains vendor name and address information. Imagine you are generating a vendor report and need to list the vendor location as part of the vendor name in the format name (location).

The report wants a single value, and the data in the table is stored in two columns: vend_name and vend_country. In addition, you need to surround vend_country with parentheses, and those are definitely not stored in the database table. The SELECT statement that returns the vendor names and locations is simple enough, but how would you create this combined value?

> **PLAIN ENGLISH: Concatenate**
> Joining values together (by appending them to each other) to form a single long value.

The solution is to concatenate the two columns. In T-SQL SELECT statements, you can concatenate columns using the + operator.

Input ▼

```
SELECT vend_name + ' (' + vend_country + ')'
FROM vendors
ORDER BY vend_name;
```

Output ▼

```
- - - - - - - - - - - - - - - - - - - - - - - - - - - - - - - - - - - - - - - - -
ACME                     (USA                      )
Anvils R Us              (USA                      )
Furball Inc.             (USA                      )
Jet Set                  (England                  )
Jouets Et Ours           (France                   )
LT Supplies              (USA                      )
```

Analysis ▼

The + operator concatenates strings, appending them to each other to create one bigger string. The previous SELECT statements concatenate four elements:

▶ The name stored in the `vend_name` column

▶ A string containing a space and an opening parenthesis

▶ The state stored in the `vend_country` column

▶ A string containing the closing parenthesis

As you can see in the output shown previously, the SELECT statement returns a single column (a calculated field) containing all four of these elements as one unit. However, because of how SQL Server stores data in fixed-length columns, the retrieved columns were all padded with spaces to their maximum length. As such, the new calculated field contains extraneous spaces and is not exactly what we were looking for.

Back in Lesson 8, "Using Wildcard Filtering," I mentioned the need to trim data so as to remove any trailing spaces. This can be done using the T-SQL `RTrim()` function, as follows:

Input ▼

```
SELECT RTrim(vend_name) + ' (' + RTrim(vend_country) + ')'
FROM vendors
ORDER BY vend_name;
```

Output ▼

```
- - - - - - - - - - - - - - - - - - - - - - - - - - - - - - - - - - - - - - - - - -
ACME (USA)
Anvils R Us (USA)
Furball Inc. (USA)
Jet Set (England)
Jouets Et Ours (France)
LT Supplies (USA)
```

Analysis ▼

The `RTrim()` function trims all spaces from the right of a value. By using `RTrim()`, you can trim the individual columns properly.

> NOTE: **The** LTrim( ) **Function**
>
> In addition to RTrim( ) (which, as you've just seen, trims the right side of a string), T-SQL also supports the use of LTrim( ) (which trims the left side of a string). To trim both the right and left sides of a string, use both functions, as in RTrim(LTrim(vend_name)).

Using Aliases

The SELECT statement used to concatenate the address field works well, as shown in the previous output. But what is the name of this new calculated column? Well, the truth is, it has no name; it is simply a value. Although this can be fine if you are just looking at the results in a SQL query tool, an unnamed column cannot be used within a client application because the client has no way to refer to that column.

To solve this problem, SQL supports column aliases. An *alias* is just that, an alternative name for a field or value. Aliases are assigned with the AS keyword. Take a look at the following SELECT statement:

Input ▼

```
SELECT RTrim(vend_name) + ' (' + RTrim(vend_country) + ')' AS
➥vend_title
FROM vendors
ORDER BY vend_name;
```

Output ▼

```
vend_title
- - - - - - - - - - - - - - - - - - - - - - - - - - - - - - - - - - - - - - - - - - - - - - - - - - -
ACME (USA)
Anvils R Us (USA)
Furball Inc. (USA)
Jet Set (England)
Jouets Et Ours (France)
LT Supplies (USA)
```

Analysis ▼

The SELECT statement itself is the same as the one used in the previous code snippet, except that here the calculated field is followed by the text AS vend_title. This instructs SQL Server to create a calculated field named vend_title containing the results of the specified calculation. As you can see in the output, the results are the same as before, but the column is now named vend_title and any client application can refer to this column by name, just as it would any actual table column.

TIP: AS **Is Optional**

Unlike in most other SQL implementations, in T-SQL the AS keyword is actually optional. As such, SELECT vend_name AS VendName and SELECT vend_name VendName accomplish the same thing. In practice, it is a good idea to always specify the AS keyword (so that you'll be used to using it when you find yourself using another DBMS).

NOTE: **Derived Columns**

Aliases are also sometimes referred to as *derived columns*, so regardless of the term you run across, the meaning is the same.

Aliases have other uses, too. Some common uses include renaming a column if the real table column name contains illegal characters (for example, spaces) and expanding column names if the original names are either ambiguous or easily misread. For example, if a table contains a column named Last Name (with a space in the column name), you'd have a very hard time using that column in SQL statements and in your application. The solution would be to use an alias, like this:

```
SELECT [Last Name] AS LastName
```

Here, [and] are used to delimit the column name, and Last Name would then be aliased as LastName.

Performing Mathematical Calculations

Another frequent use for calculated fields is performing mathematical calculations on retrieved data. Let's take a look at an example. The orders table contains all orders received, and the orderitems table contains the individual items within each order. The following SQL statement retrieves all the items in order number 20005:

Input ▼

```
SELECT prod_id, quantity, item_price
FROM orderitems
WHERE order_num = 20005;
```

Output ▼

```
prod_id     quantity     item_price
--------    ----------   ---------------------
ANV01       10           5.99
ANV02       3            9.99
TNT2        5            10.00
FB          1            10.00
```

The item_price column contains the per-unit price for each item in an order. To expand the item price (item price multiplied by quantity ordered), you simply do the following:

Input ▼

```
SELECT prod_id,
       quantity,
       item_price,
       quantity*item_price AS expanded_price
FROM orderitems
WHERE order_num = 20005;
```

Output ▼

```
prod_id    quantity    item_price              expanded_price
---------- ----------- ----------------------- --------------
ANV01      10          5.99                    59.90
ANV02      3           9.99                    29.97
TNT2       5           10.00                   50.00
FB         1           10.00                   10.00
```

Analysis ▼

The expanded_price column shown in the previous output is a calculated field; the calculation is simply quantity*item_price. The client application can now use this new calculated column just as it would any other column.

T-SQL supports the basic mathematical operators listed in Table 9.1. In addition, parentheses can be used to establish order of evaluation (also referred to as *precedence*). Refer to Lesson 7, "Advanced Data Filtering," for an explanation of precedence.

TABLE 9.1   T-SQL Mathematical Operators

Operator	Description
+	Addition
-	Subtraction
*	Multiplication
/	Division
%	Modulo (returns the remainder of a division)

TIP: **How to Test Calculations**

SELECT provides a great way to test and experiment with functions and calculations. Although SELECT is usually used to retrieve data from a table, the FROM clause may be omitted to simply access and work with expressions. For example, SELECT 3 * 2; would return 6, SELECT Trim('   abc   '); would return abc, and SELECT GetDate() uses the GetDate() function to return the current date and time. You get the idea; use SELECT to experiment as needed.

Summary

In this lesson, you learned what calculated fields are and how to create them. We used examples demonstrating the use of calculated fields for both string concatenation and mathematical operations. In addition, you learned how to create and use aliases so your application can refer to calculated fields.

LESSON 10

Using Data Manipulation Functions

In this lesson, you'll learn what functions are, what types of functions T-SQL supports, and how to use these functions.

Understanding Functions

Like almost any other computer language, SQL supports the use of functions to manipulate data. Functions are operations that are usually performed on data, usually to facilitate conversion and manipulation.

An example of a function is RTrim(), which we used in the last lesson to trim any spaces from the end of a string.

> **NOTE: Functions Are Less Portable than SQL**
>
> Code that runs on multiple systems is said to be *portable*. Most SQL statements are relatively portable, and when differences between SQL implementations do occur they are usually not that difficult to deal with. Functions, on the other hand, tend to be far less portable. Just about every major Database Management System (DBMS) supports functions that others don't, and sometimes the differences are significant.
>
> With code portability in mind, many SQL programmers opt not to use any implementation-specific features. Although this is a somewhat noble and idealistic view, it is not always in the best interests of application performance. If you opt not to use these functions, you make your application code work harder. It must use other methods to do what the DBMS could have done more efficiently.
>
> If you do decide to use functions, make sure you comment your code well, so that at a later date you (or another developer) will know exactly to which SQL implementation you were writing.

Using Functions

Most SQL implementations support the following types of functions:

- ▶ Text functions are used to manipulate strings of text (for example, trimming or padding values and converting values to upper- and lowercase).

- ▶ Numeric functions are used to perform mathematical operations on numeric data (for example, returning absolute numbers and performing algebraic calculations).

- ▶ Date and time functions are used to manipulate date and time values and to extract specific components from these values (for example, returning differences between dates and checking date validity).

- ▶ System functions return information specific to the DBMS being used (for example, returning user login information or checking version specifics).

Text Manipulation Functions

You've already seen an example of text manipulation functions in the last lesson; the RTrim() function was used to trim white space from the end of a column value. Here is another example, this time using the Upper() function:

Input ▼

```
SELECT vend_name, UPPER(vend_name) AS vend_name_upcase
FROM vendors
ORDER BY vend_name;
```

Output ▼

```
vend_name              vend_name_upcase
-------------------    ----------------
ACME                   ACME
Anvils R Us            ANVILS R US
Furball Inc.           FURBALL INC.
Jet Set                JET SET
Jouets Et Ours         JOUETS ET OURS
LT Supplies            LT SUPPLIES
```

Analysis ▼

As you can see, Upper() converts text to uppercase, and so in this example each vendor is listed twice, first exactly as stored in the vendors table and then converted to uppercase in column vend_name_upcase.

Table 10.1 lists some commonly used text manipulation functions.

TABLE 10.1 Commonly Used Text Manipulation Functions

Function	Description
CharIndex()	Returns the position of a specified character within a string
Left()	Returns characters from the left of a string
Len()	Returns the length of a string
Lower()	Converts string to lowercase
LTrim()	Trims white space from the left of a string
Replace()	Replaces characters within a string with other specified characters
Right()	Returns characters from the right of a string
RTrim()	Trims white space from the right of a string
Soundex()	Returns a string's SOUNDEX value
Str()	Converts a numeric value to a string
SubString()	Returns characters from within a string
Upper()	Converts string to uppercase

One item in Table 10.1 requires further explanation. SOUNDEX is an algorithm that converts any string of text into an alphanumeric pattern describing the phonetic representation of that text. SOUNDEX takes into account similar-sounding characters and syllables, enabling strings to be compared by how they sound rather than how they have been typed. Although SOUNDEX is not a SQL concept, T-SQL (like many other DBMSs) offers SOUNDEX support.

Here's an example using the Soundex() function. Customer Coyote Inc. is in the customers table and has a contact named Y. Lee. But what if that were a typo, and the contact actually was supposed to have been Y. Lie? Obviously, searching by the correct contact name would return no data, as shown here:

Input ▼

```
SELECT cust_name, cust_contact
FROM customers
WHERE cust_contact = 'Y. Lie';
```

Output ▼

```
cust_name                 cust_contact
----------------------    ------------------
```

Now try the same search using the Soundex() function to match all contact names that sound similar to Y. Lie:

Input ▼

```
SELECT cust_name, cust_contact
FROM customers
WHERE Soundex(cust_contact) = Soundex('Y Lie');
```

Output ▼

```
cust_name                 cust_contact
----------------------    ------------------
Coyote Inc.               Y Lee
```

Analysis ▼

In this example, the WHERE clause uses the Soundex() function to convert both the cust_contact column value and the search string to their SOUNDEX values. Because Y. Lee and Y. Lie sound alike, their SOUNDEX values match, and so the WHERE clause correctly filtered the desired data.

Date and Time Manipulation Functions

Date and times are stored in tables using special datatypes with special internal formats so they may be sorted or filtered quickly and efficiently, as well as to save physical storage space.

The format used to store dates and times is usually of no use to your applications; therefore, date and time functions are almost always used to read, expand, and manipulate these values. Because of this, date and time manipulation functions are some of the most important functions in the T-SQL language.

Table 10.2 lists some commonly used date and time manipulation functions.

TABLE 10.2 Commonly Used Date and Time Manipulation Functions

Function	Description
DateAdd()	Adds to a date (days, weeks, and so on)
DateDiff()	Calculates the difference between two dates
DateName()	Returns a string representation of date parts
DatePart()	Returns parts of a date (day of week, month, year, and so on)
Day()	Returns the day portion of a date
GetDate()	Returns the current date and time
Month()	Returns the month portion of a date
Year()	Returns the year portion of a date

Functions DateDiff(), DateName(), and DatePart() require that a date part identifier be passed to them. Table 10.3 lists the supported date parts. (You may specify the date part or an abbreviation.)

TABLE 10.3 Supported Date Parts and Abbreviations

Part	Abbreviation
day	dd or d
dayofyear	dy or y
hour	hh
millisecond	ms
minute	mi or n
month	m or mm
quarter	q or qq
second	ss or s
week	wk or ww
weekday (DatePart() only)	dw
year	yy or yyyy

For example, to obtain the days of the week that orders were placed, you could use `DatePart()` specifying weekday as the part:

Input ▼

```
SELECT order_num,
       DatePart(weekday, order_date) AS weekday
FROM orders;
```

Output ▼

```
order_num   weekday
---------   ----------
20005       5
20006       2
20007       6
20008       2
20009       7
```

Analysis ▼

`DatePart()` extracts specified date parts from a date. `DatePart(weekday, order_date)` returns the day of the week for each order_date value, as shown in the aliases weekday column.

To return named weekdays (instead of numbers), you can use the `DateName()` function in much the same way:

Input ▼

```
SELECT order_num,
       DateName(weekday, DatePart(weekday, order_date)) AS
weekday
FROM orders;
```

Output ▼

```
order_num   weekday
---------   ----------
20005       Saturday
20006       Wednesday
20007       Sunday
20008       Wednesday
20009       Monday
```

Analysis ▼

Like DatePart(), DateName() accepts a date part as its first parameter. DateName(weekday, 2) returns Monday. DateName(month, 8) returns August. By combining DateName() and DatePart(), you can return the desired output.

TIP: DatePart() **Shortcuts**

Day(), Month(), and Year() are shortcuts for DatePart(day,), DatePart(month,), and DatePart(year,), respectively.

This would be a good time to revisit data filtering using WHERE. Thus far we have filtered data using WHERE clauses that compared numbers and text, but frequently data needs to be filtered by date. Filtering by date requires some extra care and the use of special T-SQL functions.

The first thing to keep in mind is the date format used by SQL Server. Whenever you specify a date, be it inserting or updating table values or filtering using WHERE clauses, the date should be in one of the recognized formats. T-SQL supports several string representations of dates:

- ► 2006-08-17

- ► August 17, 2006

- ► 20060817

- ► 8/17/2006

Of these formats, the last should be avoided (after all, is 04/05/06 May 4th of 2006, April 5th of 2006, May 6th of 2004, or... you get the idea).

TIP: **Always Use Four-Digit Years**

Two-digit years are supported, and SQL Server treats years 00–49 as 2000–2049 and years 50–99 as 1950–1999. Although these might in fact be the intended years, it is far safer to always use a full four-digit year so that SQL Server does not have to make any assumptions for you.

As such, a basic date comparison should be simple enough:

Input ▼

```
SELECT cust_id, order_num
FROM orders
WHERE order_date = '2005-09-01';
```

Output ▼

```
cust_id      order_num
---------- -----------
10001        20005
```

Analysis ▼

This SELECT statement worked; it retrieved a single order record, one with an order_date of 2005-09-01.

But is using WHERE order_date = '2005-09-01' safe? order_date has a datatype of *datetime*. This type stores dates along with time values. The values in our sample tables all have times of 00:00:00, but that might not always be the case. What if order dates were stored using the current date and time (so you'd not only know the order date but also the time of day the order was placed)? Then WHERE order_date = '2005-09-01' fails if, for example, the stored order_date value is 2005-09-01 11:30:05. Even though a row with that date is present, it is not retrieved because the WHERE match failed.

The solution is to instruct SQL Server to only compare the specified date to the date portion of the column instead of using the entire column value. To do this, you must use the DateDiff() function. DateDiff() is used to determine the difference between two dates. Look at this example:

Input ▼

```
SELECT cust_id, order_num
FROM orders
WHERE DateDiff(day, order_date, '2005-09-01') = 0;
```

Output ▼

```
cust_id      order_num
-----------  -----------
10001        20005
```

Analysis ▼

Like DatePart() and DateName() used previously, DateDiff() requires that three parameters be passed to it. The first is the date part to compare. If you want to compare two dates by day (checking that they are the same day), then specify day. If you want to check that two dates are the same month (regardless of day of month), then specify month, and so on. The next two parameters are the dates to be compared. DateDiff() returns the difference between the two dates. A return value of 0 means that there is no difference (they match). A return value of 5 would indicate that the first date is 5 greater than the second date (5 months or 5 days, and so on, depending on the date part specified). Similarly, a value of -3 would indicate that the second date is 3 greater than the first date.

> TIP: **Always Use** DateDiff()
> When comparing dates, always use DateDiff(), and don't make assumptions about how dates are stored.

Now that you know how to use dates to test for equality, using all the other operators (introduced in Lesson 6, "Filtering Data") should be self-explanatory.

But one other type of date comparison warrants explanation. What if you wanted to retrieve all orders placed in September 2005? A simple equality test does not work because it matches the day of the month too. There are several solutions, one of which follows:

Input ▼

```
SELECT cust_id, order_num
FROM orders
WHERE DateDiff(month, order_date, '2005-09-01') = 0;
```

Output ▼

```
cust_id      order_num
----------   ----------
10001        20005
10003        20006
10004        20007
```

Analysis ▼

Here, `DateDiff()` is used to locate any orders that match `2005-09-01`, matching those that are the same month. The truth is, `2005-09-10` or `2005-09-30` or any other date in September 2005 would have worked just as well. Because the specified date part is `month`, dates will match if they are in the same month (and the day of month is ignored).

Here's another solution:

Input ▼

```
SELECT cust_id, order_num
FROM orders
WHERE Year(order_date) = 2005 AND Month(order_date) = 9;
```

Analysis ▼

`Year()` returns the year from a date (or a date time). Similarly, `Month()` returns the month from a date. `WHERE Year(order_date) = 2005 AND Month(order_date) = 9` thus retrieves all rows that have an `order_date` in year `2005` and in month `9`.

Numeric Manipulation Functions

Numeric manipulation functions do just that, manipulate numeric data. These functions tend to be used primarily for algebraic, trigonometric, or geometric calculations and therefore are not as frequently used as string or date and time manipulation functions.

The ironic thing is that of all the functions found in the major DBMSs, the numeric functions are the ones that are most uniform and consistent. Table 10.4 lists some of the more commonly used numeric manipulation functions.

TABLE 10.4 Commonly Used Numeric Manipulation Functions

Function	Description
Abs()	Returns a number's absolute value
Cos()	Returns the trigonometric cosine of a specified angle
Exp()	Returns the exponential value of a specific number
Pi()	Returns the value of pi
Rand()	Returns a random number
Round()	Returns a number rounded to a specified length or precision
Sin()	Returns the trigonometric sine of a specified angle
Sqrt()	Returns the square root of a specified number
Square()	Returns the square of a specified number
Tan()	Returns the trigonometric tangent of a specified angle

Summary

In this lesson, you learned how to use SQL's data manipulation functions, paying special attention to working with dates.

LESSON 11

Summarizing Data

In this lesson, you will learn what the SQL aggregate functions are and how to use them to summarize table data.

Using Aggregate Functions

It is often necessary to summarize data without actually retrieving it all, and SQL Server provides special functions for this purpose. Using these functions, T-SQL queries are often used to retrieve data for analysis and reporting purposes. Here are some examples of this type of retrieval:

- ▶ Determining the number of rows in a table (or the number of rows that meet some condition or contain a specific value)

- ▶ Obtaining the sum of a group of rows in a table

- ▶ Finding the highest, lowest, and average values in a table column (either for all rows or for specific rows)

In each of these examples, you want a summary of the data in a table, not the actual data itself. Therefore, returning the actual table data would be a waste of time and processing resources (not to mention bandwidth). To repeat, all you really want is the summary information.

To facilitate this type of retrieval, T-SQL features a set of aggregate functions, some of which are listed in Table 11.1. These functions enable you to perform all the types of retrieval just enumerated.

> PLAIN ENGLISH: **Aggregate Functions**
> Functions that operate on a set of rows to calculate and return a single value.

TABLE 11.1   SQL Aggregate Functions

Function	Description
Avg()	Returns a column's average value
Count()	Returns the number of rows in a column
Max()	Returns a column's highest value
Min()	Returns a column's lowest value
Sum()	Returns the sum of a column's values

The use of each of these functions is explained in the following sections.

> NOTE: **Standard Deviation**
>
> A series of standard deviation aggregate functions is also supported by T-SQL, but these functions are not covered in the lessons.

The Avg() Function

Avg() is used to return the average value of a specific column by counting both the number of rows in the table and the sum of their values. Avg() can be used to return the average value of all columns or of specific columns or rows.

This first example uses Avg() to return the average price of all the products in the products table:

Input ▼

```
SELECT Avg(prod_price) AS avg_price
FROM products;
```

Output ▼

```
avg_price
--------------------
16.1335
```

Analysis ▼

The previous SELECT statement returns a single value, avg_price, that contains the average price of all products in the products table. avg_price is an alias, as explained in Lesson 9, "Creating Calculated Fields."

Avg() can also be used to determine the average value of specific columns or rows. The following example returns the average price of products offered by a specific vendor:

Input ▼

```
SELECT Avg(prod_price) AS avg_price
FROM products
WHERE vend_id = 1003;
```

Output ▼

```
avg_price
--------------------
13.2128
```

Analysis ▼

This SELECT statement differs from the previous one only in that this one contains a WHERE clause. The WHERE clause filters only products with a vend_id of 1003; therefore, the value returned in avg_price is the average of just that vendor's products.

> CAUTION: **Individual Columns Only**
> Avg() may only be used to determine the average of a specific numeric column, and that column name must be specified as the function parameter. To obtain the average value of multiple columns, you must use multiple Avg() functions.

> NOTE: NULL **Values**
> Column rows containing NULL values are ignored by the Avg() function.

The Count() **Function**

Count() does just that: It counts. Using Count(), you can determine the number of rows in a table or the number of rows that match a specific criterion.

Count() can be used in two ways:

- ► Use Count(*) to count the number of rows in a table, regardless of whether columns contain values or NULL values.

- ► Use Count(column) to count the number of rows that have values in a specific column, ignoring NULL values.

This first example returns the total number of customers in the customers table:

Input ▼

```
SELECT Count(*) AS num_cust
FROM customers;
```

Output ▼

```
num_cust
-----------
5
```

Analysis ▼

In this example, Count(*) is used to count all rows, regardless of values. The count is returned in num_cust.

The following example counts just the customers with an email address:

Input ▼

```
SELECT Count(cust_email) AS num_cust
FROM customers;
```

Output ▼

```
num_cust
- - - - - - - - - - -
3
```

Analysis ▼

This SELECT statement uses Count(cust_email) to count only rows with a value in the cust_email column. In this example, cust_email is 3 (meaning that only three of the five customers have an email address).

> **NOTE: NULL Values**
>
> Column rows with NULL values in them are ignored by the Count() function if a column name is specified, but not if the asterisk (*) is used.

The Max() Function

Max() returns the highest value in a specified column. Max() requires that the column name be specified, as shown here:

Input ▼

```
SELECT Max(prod_price) AS max_price
FROM products;
```

Output ▼

```
max_price
- - - - - - - - - - - - - - - - - - -
55.00
```

Analysis ▼

Here, Max() returns the price of the most expensive item in the products table.

> TIP: **Using** Max() **with Nonnumeric Data**
>
> Although Max() is usually used to find the highest numeric or date value, T-SQL allows it to be used to return the highest value in any column, including textual columns. When used with textual data, Max() returns the row that would be the last if the data were sorted by that column.

> NOTE: NULL **Values**
>
> Column rows with NULL values in them are ignored by the Max() function.

The Min() Function

Min() does the exact opposite of Max(); it returns the lowest value in a specified column. Like Max(), Min() requires that the column name be specified, as shown here:

Input ▼

```
SELECT Min(prod_price) AS min_price
FROM products;
```

Output ▼

```
min_price
--------------------
2.50
```

Analysis ▼

Here, Min() returns the price of the least-expensive item in the products table.

> TIP: **Using** Min() **with Nonnumeric Data**
>
> Similar to the Max() function, T-SQL allows Min() to be used to return the *lowest* value in any columns, including textual columns. When used with textual data, Min() returns the row that would be first if the data were sorted by that column.

> **NOTE: NULL Values**
> Column rows with NULL values in them are ignored by the Min()
> function.

The Sum() Function

Sum() is used to return the sum (total) of the values in a specific column.

Here is an example to demonstrate this. The orderitems table contains the actual items in an order, and each item has an associated quantity. The total number of items ordered (the sum of all the quantity values) can be retrieved as follows:

Input ▼

```
SELECT Sum(quantity) AS items_ordered
FROM orderitems
WHERE order_num = 20005;
```

Output ▼

```
items_ordered
-------------
19
```

Analysis ▼

The function Sum(quantity) returns the sum of all the item quantities in an order, and the WHERE clause ensures that just the right order items are included.

Sum() can also be used to total calculated values. In this next example, the total order amount is retrieved by totaling item_price*quantity for each item:

Input ▼

```
SELECT Sum(item_price*quantity) AS total_price
FROM orderitems
WHERE order_num = 20005;
```

Output ▼

```
total_price
--------------------
149.87
```

Analysis ▼

The function Sum(item_price*quantity) returns the sum of all the expanded prices in an order, and again the WHERE clause ensures that just the correct order items are included.

TIP: **Performing Calculations on Multiple Columns**

All the aggregate functions can be used to perform calculations on multiple columns using the standard mathematical operators, as shown in the example.

NOTE: NULL **Values**

Column rows with NULL values in them are ignored by the Sum() function.

Aggregates on Distinct Values

The five aggregate functions can all be used in two ways:

▶ To perform calculations on all rows, you specify the ALL argument or specify no argument at all (because ALL is the default behavior).

▶ To include only unique values, you specify the DISTINCT argument.

TIP: ALL **Is the Default**

The ALL argument need not be specified because it is the default behavior. If DISTINCT is not specified, ALL is assumed.

The following example uses the Avg() function to return the average
product price offered by a specific vendor. It is the same SELECT statement
used in the previous example, but here the DISTINCT argument is used so
the average only takes into account unique prices:

Input ▼

```
SELECT Avg(DISTINCT prod_price) AS avg_price
FROM products
WHERE vend_id = 1003;
```

Output ▼

```
avg_price
--------------------
15.998
```

Analysis ▼

As you can see, in this example avg_price is higher when DISTINCT is
used because there are multiple items with the same lower price.
Excluding them raises the average price.

CAUTION: DISTINCT **Usage Restrictions**

DISTINCT may only be used with Count() if a column name is specified. DISTINCT may not be used with Count(*). Therefore,
Count(DISTINCT *) is not allowed and generates an error.
Similarly, DISTINCT must be used with a column name and not with
a calculation or expression.

TIP: **Using** DISTINCT **with** Min() **and** Max()

Although DISTINCT can technically be used with Min() and Max(),
there is actually no value in doing so. The minimum and maximum
values in a column are the same whether or not only distinct values
are included.

Combining Aggregate Functions

All the examples of aggregate functions used thus far have involved a single function. But actually, SELECT statements may contain as few or as many aggregate functions as needed. Look at this example:

Input ▼

```
SELECT Count(*) AS num_items,
       Min(prod_price) AS price_min,
       Max(prod_price) AS price_max,
       Avg(prod_price) AS price_avg
FROM products;
```

Output ▼

num_items	price_min	price_max	price_avg
14	2.50	55.00	16.1335

Analysis ▼

Here, a single SELECT statement performs four aggregate calculations in one step and returns four values (the number of items in the products table as well as the highest, lowest, and average product prices).

> TIP: **Naming Aliases**
>
> When specifying alias names to contain the results of an aggregate function, try not to use the name of an actual column in the table. Although there is nothing actually illegal about doing so, using unique names makes your SQL easier to understand and work with (and troubleshoot in the future).

Summary

Aggregate functions are used to summarize data. SQL Server supports a range of aggregate functions, all of which can be used in multiple ways to return just the results you need. These functions are designed to be highly efficient, and they usually return results far more quickly than you could calculate yourself within your own client application.

LESSON 12

Grouping Data

In this lesson, you'll learn how to group data so you can summarize subsets of table contents. This involves two new SELECT statement clauses: the GROUP BY clause and the HAVING clause.

Understanding Data Grouping

In the last lesson, you learned that the SQL aggregate functions can be used to summarize data. This enables you to count rows, calculate sums and averages, and obtain high and low values without having to retrieve all the data.

All the calculations thus far were performed on all the data in a table or on data that matched a specific WHERE clause. As a reminder, the following example returns the number of products offered by vendor 1003:

Input ▼

```
SELECT Count(*) AS num_prods
FROM products
WHERE vend_id = 1003;
```

Output ▼

```
num_prods
-----------
7
```

But what if you want to return the number of products offered by each vendor? Or products offered by vendors who offer a single product, or only those who offer more than 10 products?

This is where groups come into play. Grouping enables you to divide data into logical sets so you can perform aggregate calculations on each group.

Creating Groups

Groups are created using the GROUP BY clause in your SELECT statement. The best way to understand this is to look at an example:

Input ▼

```
SELECT vend_id, Count(*) AS num_prods
FROM products
GROUP BY vend_id;
```

Output ▼

```
vend_id      num_prods
----------   ----------
1001         3
1002         2
1003         7
1005         2
```

Analysis ▼

The preceding SELECT statement specifies two columns: vend_id, which contains the ID of a product's vendor, and num_prods, which is a calculated field (created using the Count(*) function). The GROUP BY clause instructs SQL Server to sort the data and group it by vend_id. This causes num_prods to be calculated once per vend_id rather than once for the entire table. As you can see in the output, vendor 1001 has three products listed, vendor 1002 has two products listed, vendor 1003 has seven products listed, and vendor 1005 has two products listed.

Because you used GROUP BY, you did not have to specify each group to be evaluated and calculated. That was done automatically. The GROUP BY clause instructs SQL Server to group the data and then perform the aggregate on each group rather than on the entire result set.

Before you use GROUP BY, here are some important rules about its use that you need to know:

- ▶ GROUP BY clauses can contain as many columns as you want. This enables you to nest groups, providing you with more granular control over how data is grouped.

- ▶ If you have multiple groups specified in your GROUP BY clause, data is summarized at the last specified group. In other words, all the columns specified are evaluated together when grouping is established (so you won't get data back for each individual column level).

- ▶ Every column listed in GROUP BY must be a retrieved column or a valid expression (but not an aggregate function). If an expression is used in the SELECT statement, that same expression must be specified in GROUP BY. Aliases cannot be used.

- ▶ Aside from the aggregate calculations statements, every column in your SELECT statement should be present in the GROUP BY clause.

- ▶ If the grouping column contains a row with a NULL value, NULL will be returned as a group. If there are multiple rows with NULL values, they'll all be grouped together.

- ▶ The GROUP BY clause must come after any WHERE clause and before any ORDER BY clause.

Filtering Groups

In addition to being able to group data using GROUP BY, SQL Server also allows you to filter which groups to include and which to exclude. For example, you might want a list of all customers who have made at least two orders. To obtain this data, you must filter based on the complete group, not on individual rows.

You've already seen the WHERE clause in action (introduced back in Lesson 6, "Filtering Data"). But WHERE does not work here because WHERE filters specific rows, not groups. As a matter of fact, WHERE has no idea what a group is.

So what do you use instead of WHERE? T-SQL provides yet another clause for this purpose: the HAVING clause. HAVING is very similar to WHERE. In fact, all types of WHERE clauses you learned about thus far can also be used with HAVING. The only difference is that WHERE filters rows and HAVING filters groups.

> **TIP: HAVING Supports All of WHERE's Operators**
>
> In Lesson 6 and Lesson 7, "Advanced Data Filtering," you learned about WHERE clause conditions (including wildcard conditions and clauses with multiple operators). All the techniques and options you learned about WHERE can be applied to HAVING. The syntax is identical; just the keyword is different.
>
> In fact, HAVING is so like WHERE that if you were to use HAVING without specifying a GROUP BY clause, it would actually function as a WHERE clause.

So how do you filter rows? Look at the following example:

Input ▼

```
SELECT cust_id, Count(*) AS orders
FROM orders
GROUP BY cust_id
HAVING Count(*) >= 2;
```

Output ▼

```
cust_id     orders
----------- -----------
10001       2
```

Analysis ▼

The first three lines of this SELECT statement are similar to the statements shown previously. The final line adds a HAVING clause that filters on those groups with a Count(*) >= 2, that is, two or more orders.

As you can see, a WHERE clause does not work here because the filtering is based on the group aggregate value, not on the values of specific rows.

> NOTE: **The Difference Between** HAVING **and** WHERE
>
> Here's another way to look at it: WHERE filters before data is grouped, and HAVING filters after data is grouped. This is an important distinction; rows that are eliminated by a WHERE clause are not included in the group. This could change the calculated values, which in turn could affect which groups are filtered based on the use of those values in the HAVING clause.

So is there ever a need to use both the WHERE and HAVING clauses in one statement? Actually, yes, there is. Suppose you want to further filter the previous statement so it returns any customers who placed two or more orders in the past 12 months. To do that, you can add a WHERE clause that filters out just the orders placed in the past 12 months. You then add a HAVING clause to filter just the groups with two or more rows in them.

To better demonstrate this, look at the following example, which lists all vendors who have two or more products priced at 10 or more:

Input ▼

```
SELECT vend_id, Count(*) AS num_prods
FROM products
WHERE prod_price >= 10
GROUP BY vend_id
HAVING Count(*) >= 2;
```

Output ▼

```
vend_id     num_prods
----------- -----------
1003        4
1005        2
```

Analysis ▼

This statement warrants an explanation. The first line is a basic SELECT using an aggregate function, much like the examples thus far. The WHERE clause filters all rows with a prod_price of at least 10. Data is then grouped by vend_id, and then a HAVING clause filters just those groups with a count of 2 or more. Without the WHERE clause, two extra rows would have been retrieved (vendor 1002, who only sells products priced under 10, and vendor 1001, who sells three products but only one of them is priced greater or equal to 10), as shown here:

Input ▼

```
SELECT vend_id, Count(*) AS num_prods
FROM products
GROUP BY vend_id
HAVING Count(*) >= 2;
```

Output ▼

```
vend_id      num_prods
----------   -----------
1001         3
1002         2
1003         7
1005         2
```

> CAUTION: **Not All Datatypes**
>
> HAVING and GROUP BY cannot be used with columns of type text, ntext, and image.

Grouping and Sorting

GROUP BY and ORDER BY perform different but related functions, and many users confuse the two. To help clarify when and why to use these two clauses, Table 12.1 summarizes the differences between them.

TABLE 12.1 ORDER BY Versus GROUP BY

ORDER BY	GROUP BY
Sorts generated output.	Groups rows. The output might not be in group order, however.
Any columns (even columns not selected) may be used.	Only selected columns or expression columns may be used, and every selected column expression must be used.
Never required.	Required if using columns (or expressions) with aggregate functions.

The first difference listed in Table 12.1 is extremely important. More often than not, you will find that data grouped using GROUP BY will indeed be output in group order. But that is not always the case, and it is not actually required by the SQL specifications. Furthermore, you might actually want it sorted differently than it is grouped. Just because you group data one way (to obtain group-specific aggregate values) does not mean that you want the output sorted that same way. You should always provide an explicit ORDER BY clause as well, even if it is identical to the GROUP BY clause.

> TIP: **Don't Forget** ORDER BY
>
> As a rule, any time you use a GROUP BY clause, you should also specify an ORDER BY clause. That is the only way to ensure that data is sorted properly. Never rely on GROUP BY to sort your data.

To demonstrate the use of both GROUP BY and ORDER BY, let's look at an example. The following SELECT statement is similar to the ones shown previously. It retrieves the order number and total order price of all orders with a total price of 50 or more:

Input ▼

```
SELECT order_num, Sum(quantity*item_price) AS ordertotal
FROM orderitems
GROUP BY order_num
HAVING Sum(quantity*item_price) >= 50;
```

Output ▼

```
order_num    ordertotal
----------   --------------------
20005        149.87
20006        55.00
20007        1000.00
20008        125.00
```

To sort the output by order total, all you need to do is add an ORDER BY clause, as follows:

Input ▼

```
SELECT order_num, Sum(quantity*item_price) AS ordertotal
FROM orderitems
GROUP BY order_num
HAVING Sum(quantity*item_price) >= 50
ORDER BY ordertotal;
```

Output ▼

```
order_num    ordertotal
----------   --------------------
20006        55.00
20008        125.00
20005        149.87
20007        1000.00
```

Analysis ▼

In this example, the GROUP BY clause is used to group the data by order number (the order_num column) so that the Sum(*) function can return the total order price. The HAVING clause filters the data so that only orders with a total price of 50 or more are returned. Finally, the output is sorted using the ORDER BY clause.

SELECT **Clause Ordering**

This is probably a good time to review the order in which SELECT statement clauses are to be specified. Table 12.2 lists all the clauses you have learned thus far, in the order they must be used.

TABLE 12.2 SELECT Clauses and Their Sequence

Clause	Description	Required
SELECT	Columns or expressions to be returned	Yes
FROM	Table to retrieve data from	Only if selecting data from a table
WHERE	Row-level filtering	No
GROUP BY	Group specification	Only if calculating aggregates by group
HAVING	Group-level filtering	No
ORDER BY	Output sort order	No

Summary

In Lesson 11, "Summarizing Data," you learned how to use the SQL aggregate functions to perform summary calculations on your data. In this lesson, you learned how to use the GROUP BY clause to perform these calculations on groups of data, returning results for each group. You saw how to use the HAVING clause to filter specific groups. You also learned the difference between ORDER BY and GROUP BY and between WHERE and HAVING.

LESSON 13

Working with Subqueries

In this lesson, you'll learn what subqueries are and how to use them.

Understanding Subqueries

SELECT statements are SQL queries. All the SELECT statements you have seen thus far are simple queries: single statements retrieving data from individual database tables.

> PLAIN ENGLISH: **Query**
> Any SQL statement. However, this term is generally used to refer to SELECT statements.

SQL also enables you to create *subqueries*: queries that are embedded into other queries. Why would you want to do this? The best way to understand this concept is to look at a couple examples.

Filtering by Subquery

The database tables used in all the lessons in this book are relational tables. (See Appendix B, "The Example Tables," for a description of each of the tables and their relationships.) Order data is stored in two tables. The orders table stores a single row for each order containing an order number, customer ID, and order date. The individual order items are stored in the related orderitems table. The orders table does not store customer information. It only stores a customer ID. The actual customer information is stored in the `customers` table.

Now suppose you wanted a list of all the customers who ordered item TNT2. What would you have to do to retrieve this information? Here are the steps to accomplish this:

1. Retrieve the order numbers of all orders containing item TNT2.

2. Retrieve the customer ID of all the customers who have orders listed in the order numbers returned in the previous step.

3. Retrieve the customer information for all the customer IDs returned in the previous step.

Each of these steps can be executed as a separate query. By doing so, you use the results returned by one SELECT statement to populate the WHERE clause of the next SELECT statement.

However, you can also use subqueries to combine all three queries into one single statement.

The first SELECT statement should be self-explanatory by now. It retrieves the `order_num` column for all order items with a `prod_id` of TNT2. The output lists the two orders containing this item:

Input ▼

```
SELECT order_num
FROM orderitems
WHERE prod_id = 'TNT2';
```

Output ▼

```
order_num
----------
20005
20007
```

The next step is to retrieve the customer IDs associated with orders 20005 and 20007. Using the IN clause, described in Lesson 7, "Advanced Data Filtering," you can create a SELECT statement as follows:

Input ▼

```
SELECT cust_id
FROM orders
WHERE order_num IN (20005,20007);
```

Output ▼

```
cust_id
-----------
10001
10004
```

Now, combine the two queries by turning the first (the one that returned the order numbers) into a subquery. Look at the following SELECT statement:

Input ▼

```
SELECT cust_id
FROM orders
WHERE order_num IN (SELECT order_num
                    FROM orderitems
                    WHERE prod_id = 'TNT2');
```

Output ▼

```
cust_id
-----------
10001
10004
```

Analysis ▼

Subqueries are always processed starting with the innermost SELECT statement and working outward. When the preceding SELECT statement is processed, SQL Server actually performs two operations.

First, it runs the subquery:

```
SELECT order_num FROM orderitems WHERE prod_id='TNT2'
```

That query returns the two order numbers, 20005 and 20007. Those two values are then passed to the WHERE clause of the outer query in the comma-delimited format required by the IN operator. The outer query now becomes this:

```
SELECT cust_id FROM orders WHERE order_num IN (20005,20007)
```

As you can see, the output is correct and exactly the same as the output returned by the previous hard-coded WHERE clause.

> **TIP: Formatting Your SQL**
> SELECT statements containing subqueries can be difficult to read and debug, especially as they grow in complexity. Breaking up the queries over multiple lines and indenting the lines appropriately, as shown here, can greatly simplify working with subqueries.

You now have the IDs of all the customers who ordered item TNT2. The next step is to retrieve the customer information for each of those customer IDs. Here is the SQL statement to retrieve the two columns:

Input ▼

```
SELECT cust_name, cust_contact
FROM customers
WHERE cust_id IN (10001,10004);
```

Instead of hard-coding those customer IDs, you can turn this WHERE clause into yet another subquery:

Input ▼

```
SELECT cust_name, cust_contact
FROM customers
WHERE cust_id IN (SELECT cust_id
                  FROM orders
                  WHERE order_num IN (SELECT order_num
                                      FROM orderitems
                                      WHERE prod_id = 'TNT2'));
```

Output ▼

```
cust_nam                 cust_contact
--------------------     ----------------
Coyote Inc.              Y Lee
Yosemite Place           Y Sam
```

Analysis ▼

To execute this SELECT statement, SQL Server actually had to perform three SELECT statements. The innermost subquery returned a list of order numbers that was then used as the WHERE clause for the subquery above it. That subquery returned a list of customer IDs that was used as the WHERE clause for the top-level query. The top-level query actually returned the desired data.

As you can see, using subqueries in a WHERE clause enables you to write extremely powerful and flexible SQL statements. There is no limit imposed on the number of subqueries that can be nested, although in practice you will find that performance tells you when you are nesting too deeply.

CAUTION: Single Column Only

With the notable exception of subqueries used in conjunction with EXISTS (as will be shown shortly), subquery SELECT statements can only retrieve a single column, and attempting to retrieve multiple columns will return an error.

Although generally used in conjunction with the IN operator, subqueries can also be used to test for equality (using =), non-equality (using <>), and so on.

CAUTION: Subqueries and Performance

The code shown here works, and it achieves the desired result. However, using subqueries is not *always* the most efficient way to perform this type of data retrieval, although it might be. More on this is in Lesson 14, "Joining Tables," where you will revisit this same example.

Using Subqueries as Calculated Fields

Another way to use subqueries is in creating calculated fields. Suppose you want to display the total number of orders placed by every customer in your customers table. Orders are stored in the orders table along with the appropriate customer ID.

To perform this operation, follow these steps:

1. Retrieve the list of customers from the customers table.

2. For each customer retrieved, count the number of associated orders in the orders table.

As you learned in the previous two lessons, you can use SELECT Count(*) to count rows in a table, and by providing a WHERE clause to filter a specific customer ID, you can count just that customer's orders. For example, the following code counts the number of orders placed by customer 10001:

Input ▼

```
SELECT Count(*) AS orders
FROM orders
WHERE cust_id = 10001;
```

To perform that Count(*) calculation for each customer, use Count(*) as a subquery. Look at the following code:

Input ▼

```
SELECT cust_name,
       cust_state,
       (SELECT Count(*)
        FROM orders
        WHERE orders.cust_id = customers.cust_id) AS orders
FROM customers
ORDER BY cust_name;
```

Output ▼

```
cust_name                      cust_state  orders
--------------------------     ----------  ----------
Coyote Inc.                    MI          2
E Fudd                         IL          1
Mouse House                    OH          0
Wascals                        IN          1
Yosemite Place                 AZ          1
```

Analysis ▼

This SELECT statement returns three columns for every customer in the customers table: cust_name, cust_state, and orders. orders is a calculated field that is set by a subquery provided in parentheses. That subquery is executed once for every customer retrieved. In this example, the subquery is executed five times because five customers were retrieved.

The WHERE clause in this subquery is a little different from the WHERE clauses used previously because it uses fully qualified column names (first mentioned in Lesson 4, "Retrieving Data"). The following clause tells SQL to compare the cust_id in the orders table to the one currently being retrieved from the customers table:

```
WHERE orders.cust_id = customers.cust_id
```

> PLAIN ENGLISH: **Correlated Subquery**
> A subquery that refers to the outer query.

This type of subquery is called a *correlated subquery*. This syntax, the table name and the column name separated by a period, must be used whenever there is possible ambiguity about column names. Why? Well, let's look at what happens if fully qualified column names are not used:

Input ▼

```
SELECT cust_name,
       cust_state,
       (SELECT Count(*)
        FROM orders
        WHERE cust_id = cust_id) AS orders
FROM customers
ORDER BY cust_name;
```

Output ▼

```
cust_name                     cust_state orders
---------------------------- ---------- ----------
Coyote Inc.                   MI         5
E Fudd                        IL         5
Mouse House                   OH         5
Wascals                       IN         5
Yosemite Place                AZ         5
```

Analysis ▼

Obviously the returned results are incorrect (compare them to the previous results), but why did this happen? There are two cust_id columns, one in customers and one in orders, and those two columns need to be compared to correctly match orders with their appropriate customers. Without fully qualifying the column names, SQL Server assumes you are comparing the cust_id in the orders table to itself. Also, the statement

SELECT Count(*) FROM orders WHERE cust_id = cust_id;

always returns the total number of orders in the orders table (because SQL Server checks to see that every order's cust_id matches itself, which it always does, of course).

Although subqueries are extremely useful in constructing this type of SELECT statement, care must be taken to properly qualify ambiguous column names.

NOTE: **Always More Than One Solution**

As explained earlier in this lesson, although the sample code shown here works, it is often not the most efficient way to perform this type of data retrieval. You will revisit this example in a later lesson.

Checking for Existence with Subqueries

Another use for subqueries is in conjunction with the EXISTS predicate. EXISTS, when used in a WHERE clause, looks at the results returned by a subquery, not at specific columns of data, but rather at the number of rows. If the subquery returns rows, the EXISTS test is true and the WHERE clause matches. However, if no rows are returned, the EXISTS test is false, and the WHERE clause does not match.

Look at this SELECT statement:

Input ▼

```
SELECT cust_id, cust_name
FROM customers
WHERE cust_id IN (SELECT cust_id
                  FROM orders
                  WHERE DateDiff(month, order_date,
                                 '2005-09-01') = 0
                  AND customers.cust_id = orders.cust_id);
```

Output ▼

```
cust_id      cust_name
----------   ------------------
10001        Coyote Inc.
10003        Wascals
10004        Yosemite Place
```

Analysis ▼

This SELECT statement retrieves the customer name and ID for any customers who made orders in the month of September 2005. Like the examples shown earlier in this lesson, the WHERE clause uses IN and a subquery to first select the IDs of customers who made orders the specified month, and then uses the results of that subquery to select just the desired customers from the customers table.

Now let's look at another SELECT statement that returns the exact same output:

Input ▼

```
SELECT cust_id, cust_name
FROM customers
WHERE EXISTS (SELECT *
              FROM orders
              WHERE DateDiff(month, order_date,
                            '2005-09-01') = 0
              AND customers.cust_id = orders.cust_id);
```

Analysis ▼

This WHERE clause uses EXISTS instead of IN. The subquery is much the same as the one used with IN, except that this one also matches the cust_id columns in both the customers table and the orders table so that just the customers with orders in September 2005 are retrieved. You'll notice that the subquery uses SELECT *, which is usually not allowed in subqueries, although in truth it would make no difference what columns were selected because it is not the returned data that is being used to filter customers, but the existence of any matching data.

So, which to use, IN or EXISTS? For the most part you can use either; both will let you use subqueries to filter data, and both can be negated using NOT to find rows that don't match (perhaps to find all the customers who did not order in a specific month). The biggest practical difference between the two is performance. Sometimes statements using EXISTS can be processed quicker than those using IN, which is why it is often best to experiment with both options (as well as a third option, using joins, as you will see in the next lesson).

> NOTE: **Build Queries with Subqueries Incrementally**
>
> Testing and debugging queries with subqueries can be tricky, particularly as these statements grow in complexity. The safest way to build (and test) queries with subqueries is to write the T-SQL code incrementally, in much the same way as SQL Server processes subqueries. Build and test the innermost query first. Then build and test the outer query with hard-coded data, and only after you have verified that it is working embed the subquery. Then test it again. Keep repeating these steps for each additional query. This will take just a little longer to construct your queries, but doing so saves you lots of time later (when you try to figure out why queries are not working) and significantly increases the likelihood of them working the first time.

Summary

In this lesson, you learned what subqueries are and how to use them. The most common uses for subqueries are in WHERE clauses, with IN operators, and for populating calculated columns. You saw examples of all these types of operations.

LESSON 14

Joining Tables

In this lesson, you'll learn what joins are, why they are used, and how to create SELECT statements using them.

Understanding Joins

One of SQL's most powerful features is the capability to join tables on the fly within data-retrieval queries. Joins are one of the most important operations you can perform using SQL SELECT, and a good understanding of joins and join syntax is an extremely important part of learning SQL.

Before you can effectively use joins, you must understand relational tables and the basics of relational database design. What follows is by no means a complete coverage of the subject, but it should be enough to get you up and running.

Understanding Relational Tables

The best way to understand relational tables is to look at a real-world example.

Suppose you had a database table containing a product catalog, with each catalog item in its own row. The kind of information you would store with each item would include a product description and price, along with vendor information about the company that creates the product.

Now suppose you had multiple catalog items created by the same vendor. Where would you store the vendor information (things such as vendor name, address, and contact information)? You wouldn't want to store that data along with the products for several reasons:

▶ Because the vendor information is the same for each product that vendor produces, repeating the information for each product is a waste of time and storage space.

▶ If vendor information changes (for example, if the vendor moves or the area code changes), you would need to update every occurrence of the vendor information.

▶ When data is repeated (that is, the vendor information is used with each product), there is a high likelihood that the data will not be entered exactly the same way each time. Inconsistent data is extremely difficult to use in reporting.

The key here is that having multiple occurrences of the same data is never a good thing, and that principle is the basis for relational database design. Relational tables are designed so information is split into multiple tables, one for each datatype. The tables are related to each other through common values (and thus the *relational* in relational design).

In our example, you can create two tables, one for vendor information and one for product information. The vendors table contains all the vendor information, one table row per vendor, along with a unique identifier for each vendor. This value, called a *primary key*, can be a vendor ID or any other unique value. (Primary keys were first mentioned in Lesson 1, "Understanding SQL").

The products table stores only product information, with no vendor-specific information other than the vendor ID (the vendors table's primary key). This key, called a *foreign key*, relates the vendors table to the products table, and using this vendor ID enables you to use the vendors table to find the details about the appropriate vendor.

PLAIN ENGLISH: **Foreign Key**
A column in one table that contains the primary key values from another table, thus defining the relationships between tables.

What does this do for you? Well, consider the following:

- ▶ Vendor information is never repeated, so time and space are not wasted.

- ▶ If vendor information changes, you can update a single record in the vendors table. Data in related tables does not change.

- ▶ Because no data is repeated, the data used is obviously consistent, making data reporting and manipulation much simpler.

The bottom line is that relational data can be stored efficiently and manipulated easily. Because of this, relational databases scale far better than nonrelational databases.

> PLAIN ENGLISH: **Scale**
> Able to handle an increasing load without failing. A well-designed database or application is said to *scale* well.

Why Use Joins?

As just explained, breaking data into multiple tables enables more efficient storage, easier manipulation, and greater scalability. But these benefits come with a price.

If data is stored in multiple tables, how can you retrieve that data with a single SELECT statement?

The answer is to use a join. Simply put, a join is a mechanism used to associate tables within a SELECT statement (and thus the name *join*). Using a special syntax, you can join multiple tables so a single set of output is returned, and the join associates the correct rows in each table on the fly.

> NOTE: **Maintaining Referential Integrity**
>
> It is important to understand that a join is not a physical entity; in other words, it does not exist in the actual database tables. A join is created by SQL Server as needed, and it persists for the duration of the query execution.
>
> When using relational tables, it is important that you only insert valid data into relational columns. Going back to the example, if products were stored in the products table with an invalid vendor ID (one not present in the vendors table), those products would be inaccessible because they would not be related to any vendor.
>
> To prevent this from occurring, SQL Server can be instructed to only allow valid values (ones present in the vendors table) in the vendor ID column in the products table. This is known as maintaining *referential integrity,* and it is achieved by specifying the primary and foreign keys as part of the table definitions (as will be explained in Lesson 20, "Creating and Manipulating Tables").

Creating a Join

Creating a join is very simple. You must specify all the tables to be included and how they are related to each other. Look at the following example:

Input ▼

```
SELECT vend_name, prod_name, prod_price
FROM vendors, products
WHERE vendors.vend_id = products.vend_id
ORDER BY vend_name, prod_name;
```

Output ▼

vend_name	prod_name	prod_price
ACME	Bird seed	10.00
ACME	Carrots	2.50
ACME	Detonator	13.00
ACME	Safe	50.00

```
ACME              Sling                  4.49
ACME              TNT (1 stick)          2.50
ACME              TNT (5 sticks)         10.00
Anvils R Us       .5 ton anvil           5.99
Anvils R Us       1 ton anvil            9.99
Anvils R Us       2 ton anvil            14.99
Jet Set           JetPack 1000           35.00
Jet Set           JetPack 2000           55.00
LT Supplies       Fuses                  3.42
LT Supplies       Oil can                8.99
```

Analysis ▼

In the preceding code, the SELECT statement starts in the same way as all the statements you've looked at thus far, by specifying the columns to be retrieved. The big difference here is that two of the specified columns (prod_name and prod_price) are in one table, whereas the other (vend_name) is in another table.

Now look at the FROM clause. Unlike all the prior SELECT statements, this one has two tables listed in the FROM clause: vendors and products. These are the names of the two tables that are being joined in this SELECT statement. The tables are correctly joined with a WHERE clause that instructs SQL Server to match vend_id in the vendors table with vend_id in the products table.

You'll notice that the columns are specified as vendors.vend_id and products.vend_id. This fully qualified column name is required here because if you just specify vend_id, SQL Server cannot tell which vend_id columns you are referring to (because there are two of them, one in each table).

CAUTION: **Fully Qualifying Column Names**

You must use the fully qualified column name (table and column separated by a period) whenever there is possible ambiguity about to which column you are referring. SQL Server returns an error message if you refer to an ambiguous column name without fully qualifying it with a table name.

The Importance of the WHERE Clause

It might seem strange to use a WHERE clause to set the join relationship, but actually there is a very good reason for this. Remember, when tables are joined in a SELECT statement, that relationship is constructed on the fly. Nothing in the database table definitions can instruct SQL Server how to join the tables. You have to do that yourself. When you join two tables, what you are actually doing is pairing every row in the first table with every row in the second table. The WHERE clause acts as a filter to only include rows that match the specified filter condition, the join condition, in this case. Without the WHERE clause, every row in the first table is paired with every row in the second table, regardless of whether they logically go together.

> PLAIN ENGLISH: **Cartesian Product**
> The results returned by a table relationship without a join condition.
> The number of rows retrieved is the number of rows in the first table
> multiplied by the number of rows in the second table.

To understand this, look at the following SELECT statement and output:

Input ▼

```
SELECT vend_name, prod_name, prod_price
FROM vendors, products
ORDER BY vend_name, prod_name;
```

Output ▼

vend_name	prod_name	prod_price
ACME	.5 ton anvil	5.99
ACME	1 ton anvil	9.99
ACME	2 ton anvil	14.99
ACME	Bird seed	10.00
ACME	Carrots	2.50
ACME	Detonator	13.00
ACME	Fuses	3.42
ACME	JetPack 1000	35.00

ACME	JetPack 2000	55.00
ACME	Oil can	8.99
ACME	Safe	50.00
ACME	Sling	4.49
ACME	TNT (1 stick)	2.50
ACME	TNT (5 sticks)	10.00
Anvils R Us	.5 ton anvil	5.99
Anvils R Us	1 ton anvil	9.99
Anvils R Us	2 ton anvil	14.99
Anvils R Us	Bird seed	10.00
Anvils R Us	Carrots	2.50
Anvils R Us	Detonator	13.00
Anvils R Us	Fuses	3.42
Anvils R Us	JetPack 1000	35.00
Anvils R Us	JetPack 2000	55.00
Anvils R Us	Oil can	8.99
Anvils R Us	Safe	50.00
Anvils R Us	Sling	4.49
Anvils R Us	TNT (1 stick)	2.50
Anvils R Us	TNT (5 sticks)	10.00
Furball Inc.	.5 ton anvil	5.99
Furball Inc.	1 ton anvil	9.99
Furball Inc.	2 ton anvil	14.99
Furball Inc.	Bird seed	10.00
Furball Inc.	Carrots	2.50
Furball Inc.	Detonator	13.00
Furball Inc.	Fuses	3.42
Furball Inc.	JetPack 1000	35.00
Furball Inc.	JetPack 2000	55.00
Furball Inc.	Oil can	8.99
Furball Inc.	Safe	50.00
Furball Inc.	Sling	4.49
Furball Inc.	TNT (1 stick)	2.50
Furball Inc.	TNT (5 sticks)	10.00
Jet Set	.5 ton anvil	5.99
Jet Set	1 ton anvil	9.99
Jet Set	2 ton anvil	14.99
Jet Set	Bird seed	10.00
Jet Set	Carrots	2.50
Jet Set	Detonator	13.00
Jet Set	Fuses	3.42
Jet Set	JetPack 1000	35.00
Jet Set	JetPack 2000	55.00
Jet Set	Oil can	8.99
Jet Set	Safe	50.00
Jet Set	Sling	4.49

Jet Set	TNT (1 stick)	2.50
Jet Set	TNT (5 sticks)	10.00
Jouets Et Ours	.5 ton anvil	5.99
Jouets Et Ours	1 ton anvil	9.99
Jouets Et Ours	2 ton anvil	14.99
Jouets Et Ours	Bird seed	10.00
Jouets Et Ours	Carrots	2.50
Jouets Et Ours	Detonator	13.00
Jouets Et Ours	Fuses	3.42
Jouets Et Ours	JetPack 1000	35.00
Jouets Et Ours	JetPack 2000	55.00
Jouets Et Ours	Oil can	8.99
Jouets Et Ours	Safe	50.00
Jouets Et Ours	Sling	4.49
Jouets Et Ours	TNT (1 stick)	2.50
Jouets Et Ours	TNT (5 sticks)	10.00
LT Supplies	.5 ton anvil	5.99
LT Supplies	1 ton anvil	9.99
LT Supplies	2 ton anvil	14.99
LT Supplies	Bird seed	10.00
LT Supplies	Carrots	2.50
LT Supplies	Detonator	13.00
LT Supplies	Fuses	3.42
LT Supplies	JetPack 1000	35.00
LT Supplies	JetPack 2000	55.00
LT Supplies	Oil can	8.99
LT Supplies	Safe	50.00
LT Supplies	Sling	4.49
LT Supplies	TNT (1 stick)	2.50
LT Supplies	TNT (5 sticks)	10.00

Analysis ▼

As you can see in the preceding output, the Cartesian product is seldom what you want. The data returned here has matched every product with every vendor, including products with the incorrect vendor (and even vendors with no products at all).

> CAUTION: **Don't Forget the** WHERE **Clause**
>
> Make sure all your joins have WHERE clauses; otherwise, SQL Server will return far more data than you want. Similarly, make sure your WHERE clauses are correct. An incorrect filter condition causes SQL Server to return incorrect data.

> TIP: **Cross Joins**
> Sometimes you'll hear the type of join that returns a Cartesian product referred to as a *cross join*.

In Lesson 13, "Working with Subqueries," you saw two ways to obtain a list of customers who ordered products in September of 2005, and both solutions used subqueries (one using IN and one using EXISTS). Here is a third solution, this time using an inner join:

Input ▼

```
SELECT customers.cust_id, customers.cust_name
FROM customers, orders
WHERE DateDiff(month, order_date, '2005-09-01') = 0
 AND customers.cust_id = orders.cust_id;
```

Output ▼

```
cust_id     cust_name
----------  ------------------
10001       Coyote Inc.
10003       Wascals
10004       Yosemite Place
```

Inner Joins

The join you have been using so far is called an *equijoin*, a join based on the testing of equality between two tables. This kind of join is also called an *inner join*. In fact, you may use a slightly different syntax for these joins, specifying the type of join explicitly. The following SELECT statement returns the exact same data as the preceding example:

Input ▼

```
SELECT vend_name, prod_name, prod_price
FROM vendors INNER JOIN products
 ON vendors.vend_id = products.vend_id;
```

Analysis ▼

The SELECT in this statement is the same as the preceding SELECT statement, but the FROM clause is different. Here, the relationship between the
two tables is part of the FROM clause specified as INNER JOIN. When using
this syntax, the join condition is specified using the special ON clause
instead of a WHERE clause. The actual condition passed to ON is the same as
would be passed to WHERE.

NOTE: **Output Ordering**

The WHERE syntax join and the INNER JOIN syntax join return the
exact same results. However, you may notice that the two forms of
joins return results in different orders. Of course, if you specify an
ORDER BY clause, then regardless of the syntax used, the data will
be sorted as specified.

TIP: **Which Syntax To Use?**

Per the ANSI SQL specification, use of the INNER JOIN syntax is
preferable. Although using the WHERE clause to define joins is indeed
simpler, using explicit join syntax ensures that you will never forget
the join condition, and in some cases it can impact performance, too.

Joining Multiple Tables

SQL imposes no limit to the number of tables that may be joined in a
SELECT statement. The basic rules for creating the join remain the same.
First list all the tables and then define the relationship between each. Here
is an example:

Input ▼

```
SELECT prod_name, vend_name, prod_price, quantity
FROM orderitems, products, vendors
WHERE products.vend_id = vendors.vend_id
  AND orderitems.prod_id = products.prod_id
  AND order_num = 20005;
```

Output ▼

prod_name	vend_name	prod_price	quantity
.5 ton anvil	Anvils R Us	5.99	10
1 ton anvil	Anvils R Us	9.99	3
TNT (5 sticks)	ACME	10.00	5
Bird seed	ACME	10.00	1

Analysis ▼

This example displays the items in order number 20005. Order items are stored in the orderitems table. Each product is stored by its product ID, which refers to a product in the products table. The products are linked to the appropriate vendor in the vendors table by the vendor ID, which is stored with each product record. The FROM clause here lists the three tables, and the WHERE clause defines both of those join conditions. An additional WHERE condition is then used to filter just the items for order 20005.

CAUTION: **Performance Considerations**

SQL Server processes joins at runtime, relating each table as specified. This process can become very resource intensive, so be careful not to join tables unnecessarily. The more tables you join, the more performance degrades.

This degradation can be dramatically decreased (perhaps even eliminated) by effectively creating indexes for all foreign key columns.

Now would be a good time to revisit the example from Lesson 13. As you will recall, this SELECT statement returns a list of customers who ordered product TNT2:

Input ▼

```
SELECT cust_name, cust_contact
FROM customers
WHERE cust_id IN (SELECT cust_id
                  FROM orders
                  WHERE order_num IN (SELECT order_num
                                      FROM orderitems
                                      WHERE prod_id = 'TNT2'));
```

As mentioned in Lesson 13, using subqueries might not always be the most efficient way to perform complex SELECT operations. So, as promised, here is the same query using joins:

Input ▼

```
SELECT cust_name, cust_contact
FROM customers, orders, orderitems
WHERE customers.cust_id = orders.cust_id
  AND orderitems.order_num = orders.order_num
  AND prod_id = 'TNT2';
```

Output ▼

```
cust_nam                   cust_contact
--------------------    ----------------
Coyote Inc.             Y Lee
Yosemite Place          Y Sam
```

Analysis ▼

As explained in Lesson 13, returning the data needed in this query requires the use of three tables. But instead of using them within nested subqueries, here two joins are used to connect the tables. There are three WHERE clause conditions here. The first two connect the tables in the join, and the last one filters the data for product TNT2.

TIP: **It Pays to Experiment**

As you can see, there is often more than one way to perform any given SQL operation. And there is rarely a definitive right or wrong way. Performance can be affected by the type of operation, the amount of data in the tables, whether indexes and keys are present, and a whole slew of other criteria. Therefore, it is often worth experimenting with different selection mechanisms to find the one that works best for you.

Summary

Joins are one of the most important and powerful features in SQL, and using them effectively requires a basic understanding of relational database design. In this lesson, you learned some of the basics of relational database design as an introduction to learning about joins. You also learned how to create an equijoin (also known as an *inner join*), which is the most commonly used form of join. In the next lesson, you'll learn how to create other types of joins.

LESSON 15

Creating Advanced Joins

In this lesson, you'll learn all about additional join types: what they are and how to use them. You'll also learn how to use table aliases and how to use aggregate functions with joined tables.

Using Table Aliases

Back in Lesson 9, "Creating Calculated Fields," you learned how to use aliases to refer to retrieved table columns. The syntax to alias a column looks like this:

Input ▼

```
SELECT RTrim(vend_name) + ' (' + RTrim(vend_country) + ')' AS
vend_title
FROM vendors
ORDER BY vend_name;
```

In addition to using aliases for column names and calculated fields, SQL also enables you to alias table names. There are two primary reasons to do this:

- ▶ To shorten the SQL syntax
- ▶ To enable multiple uses of the same table within a single SELECT statement

Take a look at the following SELECT statement. It is basically the same statement as an example used in the previous lesson, but it has been modified to use aliases:

Input ▼

```
SELECT cust_name, cust_contact
FROM customers AS c, orders AS o, orderitems AS oi
WHERE c.cust_id = o.cust_id
  AND oi.order_num = o.order_num
  AND prod_id = 'TNT2';
```

Analysis ▼

You'll notice that the three tables in the FROM clauses all have aliases. customers AS c establishes c as an alias for customers, and so on. This enables you to use the abbreviated c instead of the full text customers. In this example, the table aliases were used only in the WHERE clause, but aliases are not limited to just WHERE. You can use aliases in the SELECT list, the ORDER BY clause, and in any other part of the statement as well.

> NOTE: **Execution Time Only**
>
> It is worth noting that table aliases are only used during query execution. Unlike column aliases, table aliases are never returned to the client.

Using Different Join Types

So far, you have used only simple joins known as *inner joins* or *equijoins*. You'll now take a look at three additional join types: the self join, the natural join, and the outer join.

Self Joins

As mentioned earlier, one of the primary reasons to use table aliases is to be able to refer to the same table more than once in a single SELECT statement. An example will demonstrate this.

Suppose that a problem is found with a product (item ID DTNTR), and you want to know all the products made by the same vendor so as to determine whether the problem applies to them too. This query requires that you first find out which vendor creates item DTNTR and then find which other products are made by that vendor. The following is one way to approach this problem:

Input ▼

```
SELECT prod_id, prod_name
FROM products
WHERE vend_id = (SELECT vend_id
                 FROM products
                 WHERE prod_id = 'DTNTR');
```

Output ▼

```
prod_id      prod_name
---------    --------------------
DTNTR        Detonator
FB           Bird seed
FC           Carrots
SAFE         Safe
SLING        Sling
TNT1         TNT (1 stick)
TNT2         TNT (5 sticks)
```

Analysis ▼

This first solution uses subqueries. The inner SELECT statement does a simple retrieval to return the vend_id of the vendor that makes item DTNTR. That ID is the one used in the WHERE clause of the outer query, so all items produced by that vendor are retrieved. (You learned all about subqueries in Lesson 13, "Working with Subqueries." Refer to that lesson for more information.)

Now look at the same query using a join:

Input ▼

```
SELECT p1.prod_id, p1.prod_name
FROM products AS p1, products AS p2
WHERE p1.vend_id = p2.vend_id
  AND p2.prod_id = 'DTNTR';
```

Output ▼

```
prod_id    prod_name
---------- --------------------
DTNTR      Detonator
FB         Bird seed
FC         Carrots
SAFE       Safe
SLING      Sling
TNT1       TNT (1 stick)
TNT2       TNT (5 sticks)
```

Analysis ▼

The two tables needed in this query are actually the same table, so the products table appears in the FROM clause twice. Although this is perfectly legal, any references to table products would be ambiguous because SQL Server could not know to which instance of the products table you are referring.

To resolve this problem, table aliases are used. The first occurrence of products has an alias of p1, and the second has an alias of p2. Now those aliases can be used as table names. The SELECT statement, for example, uses the p1 prefix to explicitly state the full name of the desired columns. If it did not, SQL Server would return an error because there are two columns named prod_id and prod_name. It cannot know which one you want (even though, in truth, they are one and the same). The WHERE clause first joins the tables (by matching vend_id in p1 to vend_id in p2) and then filters the data by prod_id in the second table to return only the desired data.

TIP: **Self Joins Instead of Subqueries**

Self joins are often used to replace statements using subqueries that retrieve data from the same table as the outer statement. Although the end result is the same, sometimes these joins execute far more quickly than do subqueries. It is usually worth experimenting with both to determine which performs better.

Natural Joins

Whenever tables are joined, at least one column appears in more than one table (the columns being joined). Standard joins (the inner joins you learned about in the previous lesson) return all data, even multiple occurrences of the same column. A *natural join* simply eliminates those multiple occurrences so only one of each column is returned.

How does it do this? The answer is, it doesn't; you do it. A natural join is a join in which you select only columns that are unique. This is typically done using a wildcard (SELECT *) for one table and explicit subsets of the columns for all other tables. The following is an example:

Input ▼

```
SELECT c.*, o.order_num, o.order_date,
       oi.prod_id, oi.quantity, OI.item_price
FROM customers AS c, orders AS o, orderitems AS oi
WHERE c.cust_id = o.cust_id
  AND oi.order_num = o.order_num
  AND prod_id = 'FB';
```

Analysis ▼

In this example, a wildcard is used for the first table only. All other columns are explicitly listed so no duplicate columns are retrieved.

The truth is, every inner join you have created thus far is actually a natural join, and you will probably never even need an inner join that is not a natural join.

Outer Joins

Most joins relate rows in one table with rows in another. But occasionally, you want to include rows that have no related rows. For example, you might use joins to accomplish the following tasks:

▶ Count how many orders each customer placed, including customers who have yet to place an order.

► List all products with order quantities, including products not
ordered by anyone.

► Calculate average sale sizes, taking into account customers who
have not yet placed an order.

In each of these examples, the join includes table rows that have no associated rows in the related table. This type of join is called an *outer join.*

The following SELECT statement is a simple inner join. It retrieves a list of
all customers and their orders:

Input ▼

```
SELECT customers.cust_id, orders.order_num
FROM customers INNER JOIN orders
 ON customers.cust_id = orders.cust_id;
```

Outer join syntax is similar. To retrieve a list of all customers, including
those who have placed no orders, you can do the following:

Input ▼

```
SELECT customers.cust_id, orders.order_num
FROM customers LEFT OUTER JOIN orders
 ON customers.cust_id = orders.cust_id;
```

Output ▼

```
cust_id     order_num
----------  ----------
10001       20005
10001       20009
10002       NULL
10003       20006
10004       20007
10005       20008
```

Analysis ▼

Like the inner join shown in the previous lesson, this SELECT statement uses the keywords OUTER JOIN to specify the join type (instead of specifying it in the WHERE clause). But unlike inner joins, which relate rows in both tables, outer joins also include rows with no related rows. When using OUTER JOIN syntax, you must use the RIGHT or LEFT keyword to specify the table from which to include all rows (RIGHT for the one on the right of OUTER JOIN and LEFT for the one on the left). The previous example uses LEFT OUTER JOIN to select all the rows from the table on the left in the FROM clause (the customers table). To select all the rows from the table on the right, you use a RIGHT OUTER JOIN, as shown in this example:

Input ▼

```
SELECT customers.cust_id, orders.order_num
FROM customers RIGHT OUTER JOIN orders
 ON orders.cust_id = customers.cust_id;
```

> TIP: **Outer Join Types**
>
> There are two basic forms of outer joins: the left outer join and the right outer join. The only difference between them is the order of the tables they are relating. In other words, a left outer join can be turned into a right outer join simply by reversing the order of the tables in the FROM or WHERE clause. As such, the two types of outer joins can be used interchangeably, and the decision about which one is used is based purely on convenience.

NOTE: **Non-ANSI Outer Joins**

In the previous lesson, you learned two ways to write an inner join: using a simplified WHERE clause and using INNER JOIN syntax. In this lesson, you've seen the ANSI-style OUTER JOIN syntax but not a simplified WHERE clause outer join.

The truth is there is a simplified syntax for outer joins using a WHERE clause. An example is provided here so that you'll know what it is if ever you run into it (and you'll also learn why you should avoid using this syntax).

Here's the simplified outer join:

```
SELECT customers.cust_id, orders.order_num
FROM customers, orders
WHERE customers.cust_id *= orders.cust_id;
```

The *= instructs SQL Server to retrieve all the rows from the first table (customers, the table nearer the *) and only related rows from the second table (orders, the table nearer the =). Therefore, *= creates a left outer join. Similarly, =* would create a right outer join (because * is on the right).

As stated previously, it is a simpler syntax. But alas, support for this form of syntax is not part of the ANSI standard, and will not be supported in future versions of SQL Server. It is supported in SQL Server 6.x, SQL Server 7, and SQL Server 2000, and can be supported in SQL Server 2005 (support is disabled by default, but it can be enabled using sp_dbcmptlevel to enable backward compatibility), but will not be supported in the future.

As such, so as to preclude future compatibility issues, the simplified WHERE form of outer join should be avoided. This does not apply to the simplified inner join syntax (shown in the last lesson), which Microsoft has not announced any intention of dropping support for.

There is one other form of outer join worth noting, although you will likely rarely find a use for it. The FULL OUTER JOIN is used to retrieve the related rows from both tables, as well as the unrelated rows from each. (These will have NULL values for the unrelated columns in the other table.) The syntax for a FULL OUTER JOIN is the same as the previously shown outer joins, obviously substituting RIGHT and LEFT for FULL.

Using Joins with Aggregate Functions

As you learned in Lesson 11, "Summarizing Data," aggregate functions are used to summarize data. Although all the examples of aggregate functions thus far only summarized data from a single table, these functions can also be used with joins.

To demonstrate this, let's look at an example. You want to retrieve a list of all customers and the number of orders that each has placed. The following code uses the Count() function to achieve this:

Input ▼

```
SELECT customers.cust_name,
       customers.cust_id,
       Count(orders.order_num) AS num_ord
FROM customers INNER JOIN orders
 ON customers.cust_id = orders.cust_id
GROUP BY customers.cust_name,
         customers.cust_id;
```

Output ▼

```
cust_name                   cust_id      num_ord
--------------------        ----------   ----------
Coyote Inc.                 10001        2
Wascals                     10003        1
Yosemite Place              10004        1
E Fudd                      10005        1
```

Analysis ▼

This SELECT statement uses INNER JOIN to relate the customers and orders tables to each other. The GROUP BY clause groups the data by customer, and so the function call Count(orders.order_num) counts the number of orders for each customer and returns it as num_ord.

Aggregate functions can be used just as easily with other join types. See the following example:

Input ▼

```
SELECT customers.cust_name,
       customers.cust_id,
       Count(orders.order_num) AS num_ord
FROM customers LEFT OUTER JOIN orders
 ON customers.cust_id = orders.cust_id
GROUP BY customers.cust_name,
         customers.cust_id;
```

Output ▼

cust_name	cust_id	num_ord
Coyote Inc.	10001	2
Mouse House	10002	0
Wascals	10003	1
Yosemite Place	10004	1
E Fudd	10005	1

Analysis ▼

This example uses a left outer join to include all customers, even those who have not placed any orders. The results show that customer Mouse House (with no orders) is also included this time.

NOTE: **Null Value Elimination Warning**

Depending on the database client you are using, you may have seen the following warning generated by the previous T-SQL statement:

Warning: Null value is eliminated by an aggregate or other SET operation.

This is not an error message; it is just an informational warning, and it is telling you that a row (in this case, Mouse House) should have returned NULL because there are no orders. However, because an aggregate function was used (the Count() function), that NULL was converted to a number (in this case, 0).

Using Joins and Join Conditions

Before wrapping up this two-lesson discussion on joins, it is worthwhile to summarize some key points regarding joins and their use:

- ▶ Pay careful attention to the type of join being used. More often than not, you'll want an inner join, but there are often valid uses for outer joins too.

- ▶ Make sure you use the correct join condition, or you'll return incorrect data.

- ▶ Make sure you always provide a join condition, or you'll end up with the Cartesian product.

- ▶ You may include multiple tables in a join and even have different join types for each. Although this is legal and often useful, make sure you test each join separately before testing them together. This makes troubleshooting far simpler.

Summary

This lesson was a continuation of the previous lesson on joins. This lesson started by teaching you how and why to use aliases and then continued with a discussion on different join types and the various forms of syntax used with each. You also learned how to use aggregate functions with joins, and some important do's and don'ts to keep in mind when working with joins.

Combining Queries

In this lesson, you'll learn how to use the UNION operator to combine multiple SELECT statements into one result set.

Understanding Combined Queries

Most SQL queries contain a single SELECT statement that returns data from one or more tables. T-SQL also enables you to perform multiple queries (multiple SELECT statements) and return the results as a single query result set. These combined queries are usually known as *unions* or *compound queries*.

There are basically two scenarios in which you'd use combined queries:

▶ To return similarly structured data from different tables in a single query

▶ To perform multiple queries against a single table, returning the data as one query

> **TIP: Combining Queries and Multiple WHERE Conditions**
> For the most part, combining two queries to the same table accomplishes the same thing as a single query with multiple WHERE clause conditions. In other words, any SELECT statement with multiple WHERE clauses can also be specified as a combined query, as you'll see in the section that follows. However, the performance of each of the two techniques can vary based on the queries used. As such, it is always good to experiment to determine which is preferable for specific queries.

Creating Combined Queries

SQL queries are combined using the UNION operator. Using UNION, you can specify multiple SELECT statements and combine their results into a single result set.

Using UNION

Using UNION is simple enough. All you do is specify each SELECT statement and place the keyword UNION between each.

Let's look at an example. You need a list of all products costing 5 or less. You also want to include all products made by vendors 1001 and 1002, regardless of price. Of course, you can create a WHERE clause that will do this, but this time you'll use a UNION instead.

As just explained, creating a UNION involves writing multiple SELECT statements. First look at the individual statements:

Input ▼

```
SELECT vend_id, prod_id, prod_price
FROM products
WHERE prod_price <= 5;
```

Output ▼

```
vend_id      prod_id      prod_price
----------   ----------   ----------
1003         FC           2.50
1002         FU1          3.42
1003         SLING        4.49
1003         TNT1         2.50
```

Input ▼

```
SELECT vend_id, prod_id, prod_price
FROM products
WHERE vend_id IN (1001,1002);
```

Output ▼

```
vend_id      prod_id      prod_price
----------   ----------   ----------
1001         ANV01        5.99
1001         ANV02        9.99
1001         ANV03        14.99
1002         FU1          3.42
1002         OL1          8.99
```

Analysis ▼

The first SELECT retrieves all products with a price of no more than 5. The second SELECT uses IN to find all products made by vendors 1001 and 1002.

To combine these two statements, do the following:

Input ▼

```
SELECT vend_id, prod_id, prod_price
FROM products
WHERE prod_price <= 5
UNION
SELECT vend_id, prod_id, prod_price
FROM products
WHERE vend_id IN (1001,1002);
```

Output ▼

```
vend_id      prod_id      prod_price
----------   ----------   ----------
1001         ANV01        5.99
1001         ANV02        9.99
1001         ANV03        14.99
1002         FU1          3.42
1002         OL1          8.99
1003         FC           2.50
1003         SLING        4.49
1003         TNT1         2.50
```

Analysis ▼

The preceding statements are made up of both of the previous SELECT statements separated by the UNION keyword. UNION instructs SQL Server to execute both SELECT statements and combine the output into a single query result set.

As a point of reference, here is the same query using multiple WHERE clauses instead of a UNION:

Input ▼

```
SELECT vend_id, prod_id, prod_price
FROM products
WHERE prod_price <= 5
  OR vend_id IN (1001,1002);
```

In this simple example, the UNION might actually be more complicated than using a WHERE clause. But with more complex filtering conditions, or if the data were being retrieved from multiple tables (not just a single table), the UNION could have made the process much simpler.

UNION Rules

As you can see, unions are very easy to use. But a few rules govern exactly which can be combined:

- ▶ A UNION must be composed of two or more SELECT statements, each separated by the keyword UNION. (Therefore, if you were combining four SELECT statements, you would use three UNION keywords.)

- ▶ Each query in a UNION must contain the same columns, expressions, or aggregate functions, and they must be listed in the same order. (Other DBMSs do not impose this restriction and allow columns to be in any order as long as they are all present).

- ▶ Column datatypes must be compatible: They need not be the exact same type, but they must be of a type that SQL Server can implicitly convert (for example, different numeric types or different date types).

Aside from these basic rules and restrictions, unions can be used for any data retrieval tasks.

Including or Eliminating Duplicate Rows

Go back to the preceding section titled "Using UNION" and look at the sample SELECT statements used. You'll notice that when they're executed individually, the first SELECT statement returns four rows, and the second SELECT statement returns five rows. However, when the two SELECT statements are combined with a UNION, only eight rows are returned, not nine.

The UNION automatically removes any duplicate rows from the query result set (in other words, it behaves just as multiple WHERE clause conditions in a single SELECT would). Because vendor 1002 creates a product that costs less than 5, that row was returned by both SELECT statements. When the UNION was used, the duplicate row was eliminated.

This is the default behavior of UNION, but you can change this if you so desire. If you do, in fact, want all occurrences of all matches returned, you can use UNION ALL instead of UNION.

Look at the following example:

Input ▼

```
SELECT vend_id, prod_id, prod_price
FROM products
WHERE prod_price <= 5
UNION ALL
SELECT vend_id, prod_id, prod_price
FROM products
WHERE vend_id IN (1001,1002);
```

Output ▼

```
vend_id      prod_id      prod_price
----------   ----------   ----------
1003         FC           2.50
1002         FU1          3.42
1003         SLING        4.49
1003         TNT1         2.50
1001         ANV01        5.99
```

```
1001        ANV02       9.99
1001        ANV03       14.99
1002        FU1         3.42
1002        OL1         8.99
```

Analysis ▼

Using UNION ALL, SQL Server does not eliminate duplicates. Therefore, the preceding example returns nine rows, one of them occurring twice.

> TIP: UNION **Versus** WHERE
>
> The beginning of this lesson said that UNION almost always accomplishes the same thing as multiple WHERE conditions. UNION ALL is the form of UNION that accomplishes what cannot be done with WHERE clauses. If you do, in fact, want all occurrences of matches for every condition (including duplicates), you must use UNION ALL and not WHERE.

Sorting Combined Query Results

SELECT statement output is sorted using the ORDER BY clause. When combining queries with a UNION, you may use only one ORDER BY clause, and it must occur after the final SELECT statement. There is very little point in sorting part of a result set one way and part another way; therefore, multiple ORDER BY clauses are not allowed.

The following example sorts the results returned by the previously used UNION:

Input ▼

```
SELECT vend_id, prod_id, prod_price
FROM products
WHERE prod_price <= 5
UNION
SELECT vend_id, prod_id, prod_price
FROM products
WHERE vend_id IN (1001,1002)
ORDER BY vend_id, prod_price;
```

Output ▼

```
vend_id      prod_id      prod_price
---------- ---------- ----------
1001         ANV01        5.99
1001         ANV02        9.99
1001         ANV03        14.99
1002         FU1          3.42
1002         OL1          8.99
1003         FC           2.50
1003         TNT1         2.50
1003         SLING        4.49
```

Analysis ▼

This UNION takes a single ORDER BY clause after the final SELECT statement. Even though the ORDER BY appears to only be a part of that last SELECT statement, SQL Server will in fact use it to sort all the results returned by all the SELECT statements.

> NOTE: **Combining Different Tables**
> For the sake of simplicity, all the examples in this lesson combined queries using the same table. However, everything you learned here also applies to using UNION to combine queries of different tables.

Summary

In this lesson, you learned how to combine SELECT statements with the UNION operator. Using UNION, you can return the results of multiple queries as one combined query, either including or excluding duplicates. The use of UNION can greatly simplify complex WHERE clauses and retrieving data from multiple tables.

LESSON 17

Full-Text Searching

In this lesson, you'll learn how to use SQL Server's full-text searching capabilities to perform sophisticated data querying and selection.

Understanding Full-Text Searching

> NOTE: **SQL Server 2005 Only**
> This lesson covers full-text searching using SQL Server 2005. Previous versions of SQL Server do support full-text searching, but SQL Server 2005 changed and enhanced this feature so significantly that much of the content covered in this lesson won't apply to those earlier versions.

In Lesson 8, "Using Wildcard Filtering," you were introduced to the LIKE keyword, which is used to match text (and partial text) via wildcard operators. Using LIKE, it is possible to locate rows that contain specific values or parts of values, regardless of the location of those values within row columns.

But as useful as these search mechanisms are, they have several very important limitations:

- ▶ **Performance:** Wildcard matching usually requires that SQL Server try matching each and every row in a table (and table indexes are rarely of use in these searches). As such, these searches can be very time-consuming as the number of rows to be searched grows.

▶ **Explicit control:** Using wildcard matching, it is very difficult (and not always possible) to explicitly control what is and what is not matched. An example of this is a search specifying a word that must be matched, a word that must not be matched, and a word that may or may not be matched depending on whether the first word is indeed matched.

▶ **Intelligent results:** Although wildcard-based searching provides for very flexible searching, it does not provide an intelligent way to select results. For example, searching for a specific word would return all rows that contain that word, but not distinguish between rows that contain a single match and those that contain multiple matches (ranking them as potentially better matches). Similarly, searches for a specific word would not find rows that do not contain that word but do contain other related words.

All of these limitations and more are addressed by full-text searching. When full-text searching is used, SQL Server does not need to look at each row, analyzing and processing each word individually. Rather, an index of the words (in specified columns) is created by SQL Server, and searches can be made against those words. SQL Server can thus quickly and efficiently determine which words match (which rows contain them), which don't, how often they match, and so on.

Setting Up Full-Text Searching

Here's a list of requirements to perform full-text searches:

▶ Support for full-text searching must be enabled for the relevant database.

▶ A catalog must be defined (this is where full-text data is stored).

▶ A full-text index must be created for the tables and columns to be indexed.

After indexing, you can use SELECT with the FREETEXT and CONTAINS predicates to actually perform the searches.

Enabling Full-Text Searching Support

Once a database has been created, support for full text must be enabled before any full-text operations can be performed. To enable full-text support, use the sp_fulltext_database stored procedure. This stored procedure updates the currently selected database, so be sure to USE the correct database before issuing this statement:

Input ▼

```
EXEC sp_fulltext_database 'enable';
```

Analysis ▼

sp_fulltext_database accepts a parameter specifying whether to enable or disable full-text support.

> NOTE: **Using the New Database Dialog**
>
> If you use the interactive New Database dialog to create your database, you can check the Use Full-Text Indexing box, which causes the previously mentioned stored procedure to be automatically executed.

> TIP: **Not Sure If Full Text Is Enabled?**
>
> If you don't know whether full-text support is enabled, just run the stored procedure anyway. If full-text support is not enabled, the stored procedure will enable it. If full-text support is already enabled, the stored procedure will do nothing at all.

Creating a Full-Text Catalog

As already explained, SQL Server stores full-text data in a catalog (a file that needs to be created). A single catalog can be used for multiple tables and indexes, so feel free to use an existing catalog if one exists. Alternatively, just create a catalog using CREATE FULLTEXT CATALOG:

Input ▼

```
CREATE FULLTEXT CATALOG catalog_crashcourse;
```

Analysis ▼

Here, a catalog named `catalog_crashcourse` is created in the default catalog location. To specify the actual file location, the `IN PATH` attribute could have been specified.

Creating a Full-Text Index

Now that a catalog has been created, you can define the actual full-text indexes. Indexes are created using `CREATE FULLTEXT INDEX`, as seen here:

Input ▼

```
CREATE FULLTEXT INDEX ON productnotes(note_text)
KEY INDEX pk_productnotes
ON catalog_crashcourse;
```

Analysis ▼

This creates a full-text index on table `productnotes`, indexing the `note_text` column. The key with which to uniquely identify rows is required, so `KEY INDEX` is used to provide the name of the table's primary key, `pk_productnotes`. Finally, the `ON` clause specifies the catalog to be used to store full-text data, and here the just created catalog is used.

More than one column may be indexed if needed. To do this, simply specify the column names (comma delimited).

> NOTE: **Defining a Default Catalog**
>
> When `CREATE FULLTEXT CATALOG` is used to create a new catalog, the optional `AS DEFAULT` clause may be specified. Doing so makes the newly created catalog the default to be used for subsequently created full-text indexes, which would therefore mean that the final `ON` clause in `CREATE FULLTEXT INDEX` could be omitted.

Now that the full-text index has been created, any existing table data is indexed, and any data INSERT, UPDATE, and DELETE operations performed against table productnotes will force that index to be updated.

> **TIP: Don't Use Full-Text Indexes when Importing Data**
> Updating indexes takes time, not a lot of time, but time nonetheless. And updating full-text indexes takes even longer. If you are importing data into a new table, you should not enable FULLTEXT indexing at that time. Rather, first import all of the data, and then modify the table to define FULLTEXT. This makes for a much faster data import (and the total time needed to index all data will be less than the sum of the time needed to index each row individually).

Managing Catalogs and Indexes

Catalogs and indexes may be updated using ALTER FULLTEXT and dropped using DROP FULLTEXT. In practice, these statements are rarely used, with one exception. If the catalog or index becomes corrupt (returning inconsistent results) or is too slow, it may benefit from being rebuilt. You can do this as follows:

Input ▼

```
ALTER FULLTEXT CATALOG catalog_crashcourse REBUILD;
```

Analysis ▼

This statement deletes and rebuilds the catalog indexes, effectively forcing a complete reindexing.

If you would like to learn more about existing catalogs and indexes, a series of system views can be used:

Input ▼

```
SELECT * FROM sys.fulltext_catalogs;
```

Analysis ▼

This statement returns information about the currently used catalog, including physical file location and whether or not it is marked as the default catalog.

Input ▼

```
SELECT * FROM sys.fulltext_indexes;
```

Analysis ▼

This statement returns information about defined indexes, including the ID of the catalog used, whether or not the indexes are updated automatically, and when the last update started and ended.

TIP: **The** `FulltextCatalogProperty()` **Function**

A system function named `FulltextCatalogProperty()` can be used to obtain information about catalogs. `FulltextCatalogProperty()` accepts a catalog name and the property to be checked. The two most important properties are `IndexSize` and `PopulateStatus` (which lets you know if the index is up to date, currently being built, and more).

Performing Full-Text Searches

Once data has been indexed, full-text searches may be performed using two predicates:

▶ `FREETEXT` performs simple searches, matching by meaning as opposed to an exact text match.

▶ `CONTAINS` performs searches for words or phrases, taking into account proximity, derived words, and synonyms.

Both `FREETEXT` and `CONTAINS` are used in `SELECT` statement `WHERE` clauses.

Searching Using FREETEXT

FREETEXT is used to search for rows that contain words or phrases that might mean the same as (or are similar to) a specified phrase.

Let's look at an example. The following is a simple LIKE wildcard SELECT:

Input ▼

```
SELECT note_id, note_text
FROM productnotes
WHERE note_text LIKE '%rabbit food%';
```

Analysis ▼

This statement looks for the phrase rabbit food within column note_text. No rows are returned because that phrase does not appear in any rows.

Now the same search using FREETEXT full-text searching:

Input ▼

```
SELECT note_id, note_text
FROM productnotes
WHERE FREETEXT(note_text, 'rabbit food');
```

Output ▼

```
note_id    note_text
---------- -------------------------------------------------
104        Quantity varies, sold by the sack load. All
           guaranteed to be bright and orange, and suitable
           for use as rabbit bait.
110        Customer complaint: rabbit has been able to detect
           trap, food apparently less effective now.
```

Analysis ▼

FREETEXT(note_text, 'rabbit food') means "perform a FREETEXT lookup on column note_text looking for anything that could mean rabbit food." Two rows were retrieved, one containing both the words rabbit and food, but not as a joined phrase, and the other containing rabbit and a context that infers food, even though the word food is not actually present.

As you can see, FREETEXT full-text searching is very easy to use. Unfortunately, that simplicity comes at a cost, and FREETEXT searches lack the more sophisticated control you may need from full-text searching. This is why there is another predicate, named CONTAINS.

> NOTE: **Support for Other Languages**
>
> By default, FREETEXT uses the default catalog language to determine which words to index and which to ignore (words such as it and the are typically ignored because their frequency would distort results). To specify an alternate language, simply pass that language name or ID as a third parameter to FULLTEXT(). The specified language must be one of those listed in the sys.syslanguages system table. You can list the languages using the following statement: SELECT * FROM sys.syslanguages;

Searching Using CONTAINS

CONTAINS is used to search for rows that contain words, phrases, partial phrases, words with the same stem, proximity searches, synonyms (using a thesaurus lookup), and more.

Let's start with a simple example:

Input ▼

```
SELECT note_id, note_text
FROM productnotes
WHERE CONTAINS(note_text, 'handsaw');
```

Output ▼

```
note_id      note_text
----------   ---------------------------------------------
112          Customer complaint: Circular hole in safe floor
             can apparently be easily cut with handsaw.
```

Analysis ▼

`WHERE CONTAINS(note_text, 'handsaw')` means "find the word handsaw in column `note_text`."

> **TIP: CONTAINS or LIKE?**
>
> `WHERE CONTAINS(note_text, 'handsaw')` is functionality identical to `LIKE note_text = '%handsaw%'`. However, the `CONTAINS` search will typically be far quicker, especially as the size of your tables increases.

`CONTAINS` also supports the use of wildcards, as seen here:

Input ▼

```
SELECT note_id, note_text
FROM productnotes
WHERE CONTAINS(note_text, '"anvil*"');
```

Output ▼

```
note_id    note_text
---------- -----------------------------------------------------
108        Multiple customer returns, anvils failing to drop
           fast enough or falling backwards on purchaser.
           Recommend that customer considers using heavier
           anvils.
```

Analysis ▼

`'"anvil*"'` means "match any word that starts with `anvil`." Note that unlike `LIKE`, full-text searching uses * as the wildcard character (instead of %). Wildcards may be used at the beginning or end of a string.

CAUTION: **Watch Those Quotes**

The search term in the last example was `'"anvil*"'`, with the usual single quotes around `"anvil*"` (double quotes). When you pass simple text to CONTAINS, that text is then enclosed within single quotes. When you're passing wildcards, each search phrase must be enclosed within double quotes inside those outer single quotes. Failing to do this will likely cause your searches to return no matches.

CONTAINS also supports the Boolean operators AND, OR, and NOT. Here are a couple examples:

Input ▼

```
SELECT note_id, note_text
FROM productnotes
WHERE CONTAINS(note_text, 'safe AND handsaw');
```

Output ▼

```
note_id     note_text
----------  -----------------------------------------------
112         Customer complaint: Circular hole in safe floor
            can apparently be easily cut with handsaw.
```

Analysis ▼

`'safe AND handsaw'` means "match only rows that contain both safe and handsaw."

Input ▼

```
SELECT note_id, note_text
FROM productnotes
WHERE CONTAINS(note_text, 'rabbit AND NOT food');
```

Output ▼

```
note_id     note_text
----------  --------------------------------------------------
104         Quantity varies, sold by the sack load. All
            guaranteed to be bright and orange, and
            suitable for use as rabbit bait.
```

Analysis ▼

'rabbit AND NOT food' means "match only rows that contain the word rabbit and do not contain the word food."

When searching through extremely long text, you have a greater likelihood of matches being found if search terms are near each other in the saved data. A simple AND search matches terms anywhere in the text, but NEAR can be used to instruct the full-text search engine to only match terms when they are close together. Here is an example:

Input ▼

```
SELECT note_id, note_text
FROM productnotes
WHERE CONTAINS(note_text, 'detonate NEAR quickly');
```

Output ▼

```
note_id     note_text
----------  --------------------------------------------------
105         Included fuses are short and have been known to
            detonate too quickly for some customers. Longer
            fuses are available (item FU1) and should be
            recommended.
```

Analysis ▼

'detonate NEAR quickly' means "match only rows that contain the words detonate and quickly near each other."

Sometimes you may want to match a word that is part of the same family (based on the same stem). For example, if you were searching for vary, you'd also want to match varies. Obviously, a wildcard of vary* could not help here, and using var* would likely match too many false positives. This is where inflectional matching helps. Here is an example:

Input ▼

```
SELECT note_id, note_text
FROM productnotes
WHERE CONTAINS(note_text, 'FORMSOF(INFLECTIONAL, vary)');
```

Output ▼

```
note_id     note_text
---------   --------------------------------------------------
104         Quantity varies, sold by the sack load. All
            guaranteed to be bright and orange, and suitable
            for use as rabbit bait.
```

Analysis ▼

'FORMSOF(INFLECTIONAL, vary)' instructs the full-text engine to look for any words that share the same stem as the specified word (in this case, vary). As such, the row containing the word varies was matched and retrieved.

> NOTE: THESAURUS **Searches**
> FORMSOF() also supports THESAURUS searches, where words can match synonyms. To use this functionality, you must first populate an XML thesaurus file with words and their synonyms.

> TIP: **Mixing Search Types**
> So as to keep them simple and clear, the examples here use wildcards, Boolean operators, proximity searches, or inflectional searches. In truth, you can mix and match any of these as needed.

Ranking Search Results

When you perform a full-text search, the full-text engine uses sophisticated algorithms to attempt to locate what you are looking for. It can also assign a rank value to the match, the closer the match, the higher the assigned rank.

Ranks are accessed via ranking functions, FULLTEXT searches are ranked using the function FULLTEXTTABLE(), and CONTAINS searches are ranked using function CONTAINSTABLE(). Both of these functions are used the same way, and both accept search patterns (the same search patterns already explained in this lesson).

Here is an example:

Input ▼

```
SELECT f.rank, note_id, note_text
FROM productnotes,
    FREETEXTTABLE(productnotes, note_text, 'rabbit food') f
WHERE productnotes.note_id=f.[key]
ORDER BY rank DESC;
```

Output ▼

```
rank        note_id     note_text
----------  ----------  ------------------------------------------
256         110         Customer complaint: rabbit has been
                        able to detect trap, food apparently
                        less effective now.
45          104         Quantity varies, sold by the sack
                        load. All guaranteed to be bright and
                        orange, and suitable for use as
                        rabbit bait.
```

Analysis ▼

This example performs a FREETEXT-type search, but instead of filtering using the WHERE clause, it uses the FREETEXTTABLE() function and provides a search pattern instructing the full-text engine to match any rows that contain words meaning rabbit and food. FREETEXTTABLE() returns a table that is given an alias of f (to be able to refer to it in column selections and the join). This table contains a column named key, which matches the primary key of the table that was indexed (productnotes in this example), and a column named rank, which is the rank value assigned. The first row has a rank of 256 because it is a better match (it actually contains both search words), whereas the second row has a lower rank of 45 because it was a lesser match.

This technique can be used with both FULLTEXT and CONTAINS matches, but if you are performing a CONTAINS match, the function CONTAINSTABLE() should be used instead.

> NOTE: **Assigning Search Term Weights**
> The rankings assigned in this example assume that all words are equally important and relevant. If this is not the case, and some words are more important than others, then the ISABOUT() function can be used to assign weight values to specific words. The full-text search engine will then use these weight values when determining rankings.

Summary

In this lesson, you learned why full-text searching is used and how to use the T-SQL FREETEXT() and CONTAINS() functions to perform these searches. You also learned how to use Boolean operators, wildcards, proximity searches, inflectional matches, and search rankings.

LESSON 18

Inserting Data

In this lesson, you will learn how to insert data into tables using the SQL INSERT statement.

Understanding Data Insertion

SELECT is undoubtedly the most frequently used SQL statement (which is why the past 14 lessons were dedicated to it). But there are three other frequently used SQL statements you should learn. The first one is INSERT. (You'll get to the other two in the next lesson.)

As its name suggests, INSERT is used to insert (add) rows to a database table. INSERT can be used in several ways:

- ▶ To insert a single complete row
- ▶ To insert a single partial row
- ▶ To insert multiple rows
- ▶ To insert the results of a query

You'll now look at examples of each of these.

> TIP: INSERT **and System Security**
> Use of the INSERT statement can be disabled per table or per user using SQL Server security, as will be explained in Lesson 29, "Managing Security."

Inserting Complete Rows

The simplest way to insert data into a table is to use the basic INSERT syntax, which requires that you specify the table name and the values to be inserted into the new row. Here is an example of this (don't actually try this example because it will fail):

Input ▼

```
INSERT INTO Customers
VALUES(10006,
    'Pep E. LaPew',
    '100 Main Street',
    'Los Angeles',
    'CA',
    '90046',
    'USA',
    NULL,
    NULL);
```

> NOTE: **No Output**
> INSERT statements usually generate no output.

Analysis ▼

The preceding example inserts a new customer into the customers table. The data to be stored in each table column is specified in the VALUES clause, and a value must be provided for every column. If a column has no value (for example, the cust_contact and cust_email columns), the NULL value should be used (assuming the table allows no value to be specified for that column). The columns must be populated in the order in which they appear in the table definition.

So why would this INSERT statement fail as is? cust_id is an *identity field*. This means that values are assigned automatically by SQL Server, and each time a new row is added, the next unused number in sequence is automatically used and saved. By default, identity fields do not allow you to explicitly specify values; SQL Server gets to do this itself.

Even when you're not using identity fields, this previous form of INSERT is not at all safe and should generally be avoided at all costs. This type of statement is highly dependent on the order in which the columns are defined in the table. It also depends on information about that order being readily available. Even if it is available, there is no guarantee the columns will be in the exact same order the next time the table is reconstructed. Therefore, writing SQL statements that depend on specific column ordering is very unsafe. If you do so, something will inevitably break at some point.

The safer (and, unfortunately, more cumbersome) way to write the INSERT statement is as follows:

Input ▼

```
INSERT INTO customers(cust_name,
    cust_address,
    cust_city,
    cust_state,
    cust_zip,
    cust_country,
    cust_contact,
    cust_email)
VALUES('Pep E. LaPew',
    '100 Main Street',
    'Los Angeles',
    'CA',
    '90046',
    'USA',
    NULL,
    NULL);
```

Analysis ▼

This example does the exact same thing as the previous INSERT statement, but this time the column names are explicitly stated in parentheses after the table name. When the row is inserted, SQL Server will match each item in the columns list with the appropriate value in the VALUES list. The first entry in VALUES corresponds to the first specified column name. The second value corresponds to the second column name, and so on.

Because column names are provided, the VALUES must match the specified column names in the order in which they are specified, and not necessarily in the order the columns appear in the actual table. The advantage of this is that, even if the table layout changes, the INSERT statement will still work correctly. You'll notice that cust_id was not specified; unneeded columns can simply be omitted from both the columns list and the VALUES list.

The following INSERT statement populates all the row columns (just as before), but it does so in a different order. Because the column names are specified, the insertion will work correctly:

Input ▼

```
INSERT INTO customers(cust_name,
    cust_contact,
    cust_email,
    cust_address,
    cust_city,
    cust_state,
    cust_zip,
    cust_country)
VALUES('Pep E. LaPew',
    NULL,
    NULL,
    '100 Main Street',
    'Los Angeles',
    'CA',
    '90046',
    'USA');
```

> **TIP: Always Use a Columns List**
>
> As a rule, never use INSERT without explicitly specifying the column list. This will greatly increase the probability that your SQL will continue to function in the event that table changes occur.

> **CAUTION: Use VALUES Carefully**
>
> Regardless of the INSERT syntax being used, the correct number of VALUES must be specified. If no column names are provided, a value must be present for every table column. If columns names are provided, a value must be present for each listed column. If none is present, an error message will be generated, and the row will not be inserted.

Using this syntax, you can also omit columns. This means you only provide values for some columns, but not for others. (You've actually already seen an example of this; cust_id was omitted when column names were explicitly listed.)

> **CAUTION: Omitting Columns**
>
> You may omit columns from an INSERT operation if the table definition so allows. One of the following conditions must exist:
>
> ► The column is defined as allowing NULL values (no value at all).
>
> ► A default value is specified in the table definition. This means the default value will be used if no value is specified.
>
> If you omit a value from a table that does not allow NULL values and does not have a default, SQL Server generates an error message, and the row is not inserted.

> **TIP: INTO Is Optional**
>
> In T-SQL the keyword INTO is optional, so INSERT INTO customers can be shorted to INSERT customers. In practice, so as to ensure maximum portability, INTO should always be specified.

Inserting Multiple Rows

INSERT inserts a single row into a table. But what if you need to insert multiple rows? The basic INSERT statement only inserts a single row at a time, so you would need to use multiple INSERT statements. You could possibly submit them all at once, each terminated by a semicolon, like this:

Input ▼

```
INSERT INTO customers(cust_name,
   cust_address,
   cust_city,
   cust_state,
   cust_zip,
   cust_country)
VALUES('Pep E. LaPew',
   '100 Main Street',
   'Los Angeles',
   'CA',
   '90046',
   'USA');
INSERT INTO customers(cust_name,
   cust_address,
   cust_city,
   cust_state,
   cust_zip,
   cust_country)
VALUES('M. Martian',
   '42 Galaxy Way',
   'New York',
   'NY',
   '11213',
   'USA');
```

> NOTE: **One Set of** VALUES **Only**
>
> Unlike some other DBMSs, SQL Server does not support multiple VALUES clauses for a single INSERT statement.

Inserting Retrieved Data

INSERT is generally used to add a row to a table using specified values. Another form of INSERT can be used to insert the result of a SELECT statement into a table. This is known as INSERT SELECT, and, as its name suggests, it is made up of an INSERT statement and a SELECT statement.

Suppose you want to merge a list of customers from another table into your customers table. Instead of reading one row at a time and inserting it with INSERT, you can do the following:

> NOTE: **Instructions Needed for the Next Example**
> The following example imports data from a table named custnew into the customers table. To try this example, create and populate the custnew table first. The format of the custnew table should be the same as the customers table described in Appendix B, "The Example Tables." When populating custnew, be sure not to use cust_id values that were already used in customers. (The subsequent INSERT operation will fail if primary key values are duplicated.) Alternatively, just omit that column and have SQL Server generate new values during the import process.

Input ▼

```
INSERT INTO customers(cust_contact,
    cust_email,
    cust_name,
    cust_address,
    cust_city,
    cust_state,
    cust_zip,
    cust_country)
SELECT cust_contact,
    cust_email,
    cust_name,
    cust_address,
    cust_city,
    cust_state,
    cust_zip,
    cust_country
FROM custnew;
```

Analysis ▼

This example uses INSERT SELECT to import all the data from custnew into customers. Instead of listing the VALUES to be inserted, the SELECT statement retrieves them from custnew. Each column in the SELECT corresponds to a column in the specified columns list. How many rows will this statement insert? That depends on how many rows are in the custnew table. If the table is empty, no rows will be inserted (and no error will be generated because the operation is still valid). If the table does, in fact, contain data, all that data is inserted into customers.

TIP: **Column Names in** INSERT SELECT

This example uses the same column names in both the INSERT and SELECT statements for simplicity's sake. But there is no requirement that the column names match. In fact, SQL Server does not even pay attention to the column names returned by the SELECT. Rather, the column position is used, so the first column in the SELECT (regardless of its name) will be used to populate the first specified table column, and so on. This is very useful when you are importing data from tables that use different column names.

The SELECT statement used in an INSERT SELECT can include a WHERE clause to filter the data to be inserted.

Another way to insert retrieved data is to use SELECT INTO. This variation to SELECT allows you to specify a destination table that will be populated with the results of a SELECT statement.

Input ▼

```
SELECT cust_contact,
    cust_email,
    cust_name,
    cust_address,
    cust_city,
    cust_state,
    cust_zip,
    cust_country
INTO customersExport
FROM customers;
```

Analysis ▼

When used, the INTO clause must come after the column list and before the FROM clause. INTO specifies the name of a table to be created, and this table name must not already exist (or an error will be generated). Once the statement has been executed, the newly created table will contain the rows retrieved by the SELECT statement.

SELECT INTO is very useful when you're trying to create a single table that contains rows retrieved from multiple tables.

> TIP: INSERT SELECT **Versus** SELECT INTO
> You can think of INSERT SELECT as being an import operation and SELECT INTO as being an export operation.

> NOTE: **More Examples**
> Looking for more examples of INSERT use? See the sample table population scripts (described in Appendix B) used to create the sample tables used in this book.

Summary

In this lesson, you learned how to use INSERT to insert rows into a database table. You learned several other ways to use INSERT, and why explicit column specification is preferred. You also learned how to use INSERT SELECT to import rows from another table, and SELECT INTO to export rows to a new table. In the next lesson, you'll learn how to use UPDATE and DELETE to further manipulate table data.

LESSON 19

Updating and Deleting Data

In this lesson, you will learn how to use the UPDATE and DELETE statements to enable you to further manipulate your table data.

Updating Data

To update (modify) data in a table, you use the UPDATE statement. UPDATE can be used in two ways:

- ▶ To update specific rows in a table
- ▶ To update all rows in a table

CAUTION: **Don't Omit the** WHERE **Clause**
Special care must be exercised when using UPDATE because it is all too easy to mistakenly update every row in your table. Be sure to read this entire section on UPDATE before using this statement.

TIP: UPDATE **and Security**
Use of the UPDATE statement can be restricted and controlled. More on this in Lesson 29, "Managing Security."

The UPDATE statement is very easy to use; some would say too easy. The basic format of an UPDATE statement is made up of three parts:

- ▶ The table to be updated

- ▶ The column names and their new values

- ▶ The filter condition that determines which rows should be updated

Let's take a look at a simple example. Customer 10005 now has an email address, and so his record needs updating. The following statement performs this update:

Input ▼

```
UPDATE customers
SET cust_email = 'elmer@fudd.com'
WHERE cust_id = 10005;
```

The UPDATE statement always begins with the name of the table being updated. In this example, it is the customers table. The SET command is then used to assign the new value to a column. As used here, the SET clause sets the cust_email column to the specified value:

```
SET cust_email = 'elmer@fudd.com'
```

The UPDATE statement finishes with a WHERE clause that tells SQL Server which row to update. Without a WHERE clause, SQL Server would update all the rows in the customers table with this new email address, definitely not the desired effect.

Updating multiple columns requires a slightly different syntax:

Input ▼

```
UPDATE customers
SET cust_name = 'The Fudds',
    cust_email = 'elmer@fudd.com'
WHERE cust_id = 10005;
```

When updating multiple columns, you use only a single SET command and separate each column = value pair by a comma. (No comma is specified after the last column.) In this example, the columns cust_name and cust_email will both be updated for customer 10005.

> TIP: **Using Subqueries in an** UPDATE **Statement**
> Subqueries may be used in UPDATE statements, enabling you to update columns with data retrieved with a SELECT statement. Refer back to Lesson 13, "Working with Subqueries," for more information on subqueries and their uses.

To delete a column's value, you can set it to NULL (assuming the table is defined to allow NULL values). You can do this as follows:

Input ▼

```
UPDATE customers
SET cust_email = NULL
WHERE cust_id = 10005;
```

Here, the NULL keyword is used to save no value to the cust_email column.

Deleting Data

To delete (remove) data from a table, you use the DELETE statement. DELETE can be used in two ways:

- ▶ To delete specific rows from a table
- ▶ To delete all rows from a table

> CAUTION: **Don't Omit the** WHERE **Clause**
> Special care must be exercised when using DELETE because it is all too easy to mistakenly delete every row from your table. Be sure to read this entire section on DELETE before using this statement.

> TIP: DELETE **and Security**
> Use of the DELETE statement can be restricted and controlled. More on this in Lesson 29.

I already stated that UPDATE is very easy to use. The good (and bad) news is that DELETE is even easier to use.

The following statement deletes a single row from the customers table:

Input ▼

```
DELETE FROM customers
WHERE cust_id = 10006;
```

This statement should be self-explanatory. DELETE FROM requires that you specify the name of the table from which the data is to be deleted. The WHERE clause filters which rows are to be deleted. In this example, only customer 10006 will be deleted. If the WHERE clause were omitted, this statement would have deleted every customer in the table.

DELETE takes no column names or wildcard characters. DELETE deletes entire rows, not columns. To delete specific columns, use an UPDATE statement (as shown earlier in this lesson).

> NOTE: **Table Contents, Not Tables**
> The DELETE statement deletes rows from tables, even all rows from tables. But DELETE never deletes the table itself.

Guidelines for Updating and Deleting Data

The UPDATE and DELETE statements used in the previous sections all have WHERE clauses, and there is a very good reason for this. If you omit the WHERE clause, the UPDATE or DELETE is applied to every row in the table. In other words, if you execute an UPDATE without a WHERE clause, every row in the table is updated with the new values. Similarly, if you execute DELETE without a WHERE clause, all the contents of the table are deleted.

Here are some best practices that many SQL programmers follow:

▶ Never execute an UPDATE or a DELETE without a WHERE clause, unless you really do intend to update and delete every row.

▶ Make sure every table has a primary key (refer back to Lesson 14, "Joining Tables," if you have forgotten what this is), and use it as the WHERE clause whenever possible. (You may specify individual primary keys, multiple values, or value ranges.)

▶ Before you use a WHERE clause with an UPDATE or a DELETE, first test it with a SELECT to make sure it is filtering the right records; it is far too easy to write incorrect WHERE clauses.

▶ Use database-enforced referential integrity (refer back to Lesson 14 for this one, too) so that SQL Server will not allow the deletion of rows that have data in other tables related to them.

CAUTION: **Use with Caution**

The bottom line is that SQL Server has no Undo button. Be very careful using UPDATE and DELETE; otherwise, you'll find yourself updating and deleting the wrong data.

Summary

In this lesson, you learned how to use the UPDATE and DELETE statements to manipulate the data in your tables. You learned the syntax for each of these statements, as well as the inherent dangers they expose. You also learned why WHERE clauses are so important in UPDATE and DELETE statements, and you were given guidelines to follow to help ensure your data does not get damaged inadvertently.

LESSON 20

Creating and Manipulating Tables

In this lesson, you'll learn the basics of table creation, alteration, and deletion.

Creating Tables

T-SQL statements are not used just for table data manipulation. Indeed, T-SQL can be used to perform all database and table operations, including the creation and manipulation of tables themselves.

There are generally two ways to create database tables:

- ▶ Using an administration tool (such as one of the tools discussed in Lesson 2, "Introducing SQL Server") to create and manage database tables interactively

- ▶ Using T-SQL statements to manipulate tables directly

To create tables programmatically, you use the CREATE TABLE SQL statement. It is worth noting that when you use interactive tools, you are actually using T-SQL statements. Instead of you writing these statements, however, the interface generates and executes the T-SQL seamlessly for you. (The same is true for changes to existing tables.)

> NOTE: **Additional Examples**
> For additional examples of table-creation scripts, see the code used to create the sample tables used in this book.

Basic Table Creation

To create a table using CREATE TABLE, you must specify the following information:

- ▶ The name of the new table, after the keywords CREATE TABLE

- ▶ The name and definition of the table columns, separated by commas

The CREATE TABLE statement may also include other keywords and options, but at a minimum you need the table name and column details. The following T-SQL statement creates the customers table used throughout this book:

Input ▼

```
CREATE TABLE customers
(
    cust_id      INT         NOT NULL IDENTITY(1,1),
    cust_name    NCHAR(50)   NOT NULL ,
    cust_address NCHAR(50)   NULL ,
    cust_city    NCHAR(50)   NULL ,
    cust_state   NCHAR(5)    NULL ,
    cust_zip     NCHAR(10)   NULL ,
    cust_country NCHAR(50)   NULL ,
    cust_contact NCHAR(50)   NULL ,
    cust_email   NCHAR(255)  NULL ,
    PRIMARY KEY (cust_id)
);
```

Analysis ▼

As you can see in the preceding statement, the table name is specified immediately following the CREATE TABLE keywords. The actual table definition (all the columns) is enclosed within parentheses. The columns themselves are separated by commas. This particular table is made up of nine columns. Each column definition starts with the column name (which must be unique within the table), followed by the column's datatype. (Refer to Lesson 1, "Understanding SQL," for an explanation of datatypes. In addition, Appendix D, "T-SQL Datatypes," lists the datatypes supported by SQL Server.) The table's primary key may be specified at table-creation time using the PRIMARY KEY keywords; here, column cust_id is specified as the primary key column. The entire statement is terminated with a semicolon after the closing parenthesis. (Ignore the IDENTITY keyword for now; we'll come back to that later.)

TIP: **Statement Formatting**

As you will recall, white space is ignored in T-SQL statements. Statements can be typed on one long line or broken up over many lines. It makes no difference at all. This enables you to format your SQL as best suits you. The preceding CREATE TABLE statement is a good example of T-SQL statement formatting; the code is specified over multiple lines, with the column definitions indented for easier reading and editing. Formatting your T-SQL in this way is entirely optional, but highly recommended.

TIP: **Handling Existing Tables**

When you create a new table, the table name specified must not exist; otherwise, you'll generate an error. To prevent accidental overwriting, SQL Server requires that you first manually remove a table (see later sections for details) and then re-create it, rather than just overwriting it.

Working with NULL Values

Back in Lesson 6, "Filtering Data," you learned that a NULL value is no value or the lack of a value. A column that allows NULL values also allows rows to be inserted with no value at all in that column. A column that does not allow NULL values does not accept rows with no value; in other words, that column will always be required when rows are inserted or updated.

Every table column is either a NULL column or a NOT NULL column, and that state is specified in the table definition at creation time. Take a look at the following example:

Input ▼

```
CREATE TABLE orders
(
  order_num  INT       NOT NULL IDENTITY(1,1),
  order_date DATETIME NOT NULL ,
  cust_id    INT       NOT NULL ,
  PRIMARY KEY (order_num)
);
```

Analysis ▼

This statement creates the orders table used throughout this book. orders contains three columns: the order number, order date, and customer ID. All three columns are required, so each contains the keyword NOT NULL. This will prevent the insertion of columns with no value. If someone tries to insert no value, an error will be returned, and the insertion will fail.

CAUTION: **Understanding** NULL

Don't confuse NULL values with empty strings. A NULL value is the lack of a value; it is not an empty string. If you were to specify ' ' (two single quotes with nothing in between them), that would be allowed in a NOT NULL column. An empty string is a valid value; it is not no value. NULL values are specified with the keyword NULL, not with an empty string.

Primary Keys Revisited

As already explained, primary key values must be unique. That is, every row in a table must have a unique primary key value. If a single column is used for the primary key, it must be unique; if multiple columns are used, the combination of them must be unique.

The CREATE TABLE examples seen thus far use a single column as the primary key. The primary key is thus defined using a statement such as

```
PRIMARY KEY (vend_id)
```

To create a primary key made up of multiple columns, simply specify the column names as a comma-delimited list, as shown in this example:

Input ▼

```
CREATE TABLE orderitems
(
  order_num   INT        NOT NULL ,
  order_item  INT        NOT NULL ,
  prod_id     NCHAR(10)  NOT NULL ,
  quantity    INT        NOT NULL ,
  item_price  MONEY      NOT NULL ,
  PRIMARY KEY (order_num, order_item)
);
```

The orderitems table contains the order specifics for each order in the orders table. There may be multiple items per order, but each order will only ever have one first item, one second item, and so on. As such, the combination of order number (column order_num) and order item (column order_item) is unique, and thus suitable to be the primary key, which is defined as follows:

```
PRIMARY KEY (order_num, order_item)
```

Primary keys may be defined at table-creation time (as seen here) or after table creation (as will be discussed later in this lesson).

> TIP: **Primary Keys and** NULL **Values**
> Back in Lesson 1, you learned that primary keys are columns whose values uniquely identify every row in a table. Only columns that do not allow NULL values can be used in primary keys. Columns that allow no value at all cannot be used as unique identifiers.

Using IDENTITY

Let's take a look at the customers and orders tables again. Customers in the customers table are uniquely identified by column cust_id, a unique number for each and every customer. Similarly, orders in the orders table each have a unique order number stored in the column order_num.

These numbers have no special significance, other than the fact that they are unique. When a new customer or order is added, a new customer ID or order number is needed. The numbers can be anything, as long as they are unique.

Obviously, the simplest number to use would be whatever comes next, whatever is one higher than the current highest number. For example, if the highest `cust_id` is `10005`, the next customer inserted into the table could have a `cust_id` of `10006`.

Simple, right? Well, not really. How would you determine the next number to be used? You could, of course, use a `SELECT` statement to get the highest number, using the `Max()` function introduced in Lesson 11, "Summarizing Data," and then add 1 to it. But that would not be safe (you'd need to find a way to ensure that no one else inserted a row in between the time that you performed the `SELECT` and the `INSERT`, a legitimate possibility in multiuser applications). Nor would it be efficient (performing additional T-SQL operations is never ideal).

And that's where `IDENTITY` comes in. Look at the following line (part of the `CREATE TABLE` statement used to create the `customers` table):

```
cust_id      INT       NOT NULL IDENTITY(1,1),
```

`IDENTITY` tells SQL Server that this column is to be automatically incremented each time a row is added. Each time an `INSERT` operation is performed, SQL Server automatically increments the column, assigning it the next available value. This way, each row is assigned a unique `cust_id`, which is then used as the primary key value.

`IDENTITY` needs to know the number to start from (known as the *seed*) and the increment to be used each time a new value is generated. `IDENTITY(1,1)` means "start with a seed of 1 and increment by 1 to generate each new number." To start with a seed of 100 and increment by 10, you could use `IDENTITY(100,10)`. If the seed and increment values are not provided, `(1,1)` is used by default.

Only one `IDENTITY` column is allowed per table, and `IDENTITY` columns are usually used as primary keys.

NOTE: **Overriding** IDENTITY

Need to use a specific value in a column designated as IDENTITY? You can, but first you'll need to SET IDENTITY_INSERT to ON as mentioned in Lesson 18, "Inserting Data." (See the table-population scripts used in this book for examples of this.)

TIP: **Determining the** IDENTITY **Value**

One downside of having SQL Server generate (via IDENTITY) primary keys for you is that you don't know what those values are.

Consider this scenario: You are adding a new order. This requires creating a single row in the orders table and then a row for each item ordered in the orderitems table. The order_num is stored along with the order details in orderitems. This is how the orders and orderitems table are related to each other. And that obviously requires that you know the generated order_num after the orders row was inserted and before the orderitems rows are inserted.

So how could you obtain this value when an IDENTITY column is used? By referring to the special @@IDENTITY system function, like this:

SELECT @@IDENTITY AS newId;

This returns the last generated IDENTITY value as newId, which you can then use in subsequent T-SQL statements.

Specifying Default Values

SQL Server enables you to specify default values to be used if no value is specified when a row is inserted. Default values are specified using the DEFAULT keyword in the column definitions in the CREATE TABLE statement.

Look at the following example:

Input ▼

```
CREATE TABLE orderitems
(
  order_num  INT        NOT NULL ,
  order_item INT        NOT NULL ,
  prod_id    NCHAR(10)  NOT NULL ,
  quantity   INT        NOT NULL  DEFAULT 1,
  item_price MONEY      NOT NULL ,
  PRIMARY KEY (order_num, order_item)
);
```

Analysis ▼

This statement creates the orderitems table, which contains the individual items that make up an order. (The order itself is stored in the orders table.) The quantity column contains the quantity for each item in an order. In this example, adding the text DEFAULT 1 to the column description instructs SQL Server to use a quantity of 1 if no quantity is specified.

The previous example used a fixed value as the specified DEFAULT. You can also use T-SQL functions as default values, as shown in this example:

Input ▼

```
CREATE TABLE orders
(
  order_num  INT       NOT NULL  IDENTITY(1,1),
  order_date DATETIME NOT NULL  DEFAULT GetDate(),
  cust_id    INT       NOT NULL ,
  PRIMARY KEY (order_num)
);
```

Analysis ▼

Orders are stored in the orders table, and the order date is stored in the order_date column. The default value for this column is GetDate(), a T-SQL function that returns the current system date. This way, if an explicit order_date value is not specified when a row is inserted, the current date will be used automatically.

By the way, despite its name, GetDate() actually returns the current system date and time. If you want to see exactly what GetDate() returns, try the following simple SELECT statement:

Input ▼

```
SELECT GetDate();
```

> TIP: **Using** DEFAULT **Instead of** NULL **Values**
>
> Many database developers use DEFAULT values instead of NULL columns, especially in columns that will be used in calculations or data groupings.

Updating Tables

To update table definitions, you use the ALTER TABLE statement. But, ideally, tables should never be altered after they contain data. You should spend sufficient time anticipating future needs during the table-design process so extensive changes are not required later on.

To change a table using ALTER TABLE, you must specify the following information:

▶ The name of the table to be altered after the keywords ALTER TABLE. (The table must exist, or an error will be generated.)

▶ The list of changes to be made.

The following example adds a column to a table:

Input ▼

```
ALTER TABLE vendors
ADD vend_phone CHAR(20);
```

Analysis ▼

This statement adds a column named vend_phone to the vendors table. The datatype must be specified.

To remove this newly added column, you can do the following:

Input ▼

```
ALTER TABLE vendors
DROP COLUMN vend_phone;
```

One common use for ALTER TABLE is to define foreign keys. The following is the code used to define the foreign keys used by the tables in this book:

Input ▼

```
ALTER TABLE orderitems
ADD CONSTRAINT fk_orderitems_orders FOREIGN KEY (order_num)
REFERENCES orders (order_num);

ALTER TABLE orderitems
ADD CONSTRAINT fk_orderitems_products FOREIGN KEY (prod_id)
REFERENCES products (prod_id);

ALTER TABLE orders
ADD CONSTRAINT fk_orders_customers FOREIGN KEY (cust_id)
REFERENCES customers (cust_id);

ALTER TABLE products
ADD CONSTRAINT fk_products_vendors FOREIGN KEY (vend_id)
REFERENCES vendors (vend_id);

ALTER TABLE productnotes
ADD CONSTRAINT fk_productnotes_products FOREIGN KEY (prod_id)
REFERENCES products (prod_id);
```

Analysis ▼

Here, five ALTER TABLE statements are used because five different tables are being altered. Each of the statements defines a foreign key. If we had needed multiple foreign keys on a single table, those could all have been defined using a single ALTER TABLE statement.

Complex table structure changes may require a manual move process involving these steps:

1. Create a new table with the new column layout.

2. Use the INSERT SELECT or SELECT INTO statement (see Lesson 18 for details of this statement) to copy the data from the old table to the new table. Use conversion functions and calculated fields, if needed.

3. Verify that the new table contains the desired data.

4. Rename the old table (or delete it, if you are really brave).

5. Rename the new table with the name previously used by the old table.

6. Re-create any triggers, stored procedures, indexes, and foreign keys as needed.

CAUTION: **Use** ALTER TABLE **Carefully**

Use ALTER TABLE with extreme caution, and be sure you have a complete set of backups (both schema and data) before proceeding. Database table changes cannot be undone, and if you add columns you don't need, you might not be able to remove them. Similarly, if you drop a column that you do need, you might lose all the data in that column.

Deleting Tables

Deleting tables (actually removing the entire table, not just the contents) is very easy, arguably too easy. Tables are deleted using the DROP TABLE statement:

Input ▼

```
DROP TABLE customers2;
```

Analysis ▼

This statement deletes the `customers2` table (assuming it exists). There is no confirmation, nor is there an undo: Executing the statement will permanently remove the table.

Renaming Tables

There is no T-SQL statement for renaming tables, but a SQL Server–provided stored procedure named `sp_rename` can be used to accomplish this:

Input ▼

```
EXEC sp_rename 'customers2', 'customers';
```

Analysis ▼

`sp_rename` can be used to rename all sorts of objects, including tables. This example renames table `customers2` to `customers`.

Summary

In this lesson, you learned several new SQL statements. `CREATE TABLE` is used to create new tables, `ALTER TABLE` is used to change table columns (or other objects such as constraints and indexes), and `DROP TABLE` is used to completely delete a table. These statements should be used with extreme caution, and only after backups have been made. You also learned about identity fields, defining primary and foreign keys, and other important table and column options.

LESSON 21

Using Views

In this lesson, you'll learn exactly what views are, how they work, and when they should be used. You'll also see how views can be used to simplify some of the SQL operations performed in earlier lessons.

Understanding Views

Views are virtual tables. Unlike tables that contain data, views simply contain queries that dynamically retrieve data when used.

The best way to understand views is to look at an example. Back in Lesson 14, "Joining Tables," you used the following SELECT statement to retrieve data from three tables:

Input ▼

```
SELECT cust_name, cust_contact
FROM customers, orders, orderitems
WHERE customers.cust_id = orders.cust_id
  AND orderitems.order_num = orders.order_num
  AND prod_id = 'TNT2';
```

That query was used to retrieve the customers who had ordered a specific product. Anyone needing this data would have to understand the table structure as well as how to create the query and join the tables. To retrieve the same data for another product (or for multiple products), you would have to modify the last WHERE clause.

Now imagine that you could wrap that entire query in a virtual table called productcustomers. You could then simply do the following to retrieve the same data:

Input ▼

```
SELECT cust_name, cust_contact
FROM productcustomers
WHERE prod_id = 'TNT2';
```

This is where views come into play. productcustomers is a view, and as a view, it does not contain any actual columns or data as a table would. Instead, it contains a SQL query; the same query used previously to join the tables properly.

Why Use Views

You've already seen one use for views. Here are some other common uses:

- ► To reuse SQL statements.

- ► To simplify complex SQL operations. After the query is written, it can be reused easily, without you having to know the details of the underlying query itself.

- ► To expose parts of a table instead of complete tables.

- ► To secure data. Users can be given access to specific subsets of tables instead of to entire tables.

- ► To change data formatting and representation. Views can return data formatted and presented differently from their underlying tables.

For the most part, after views are created, they can be used in the same way as tables. You can perform SELECT operations, filter and sort data, join views to other views or tables, and even add and update data (with some restrictions, as will be noted later in this lesson).

The important thing to remember is, views are just that, views into data stored elsewhere. Views contain no data themselves, so the data they return is retrieved from other tables. When data is added or changed in those tables, the views will return that changed data.

View Rules and Restrictions

Here are some of the most common rules and restrictions governing view creation and usage:

- ▶ Like tables, views must be uniquely named. (They cannot have the name of any other table or view.)

- ▶ There is no limit to the number of views that can be created.

- ▶ SQL Server views may contain no more than 1,024 columns.

- ▶ To create views, you must have security access. This is usually granted by the database administrator.

- ▶ Views can be nested; that is, a view may be built using a query that retrieves data from another view.

- ▶ ORDER BY may not be used in views, but ORDER BY may be used in the SELECT statement that retrieves data from the view.

- ▶ Views cannot be indexed, nor can they have triggers or default values associated with them.

- ▶ Views can be used in conjunction with tables (for example, to create a SELECT statement that joins a table and a view).

Using Views

So now that you know what views are (and the rules and restrictions that govern them), let's look at view creation:

- ▶ Views are created using the CREATE VIEW statement.

- ▶ To remove a view, you use the DROP statement. The syntax is simply DROP VIEW viewname;.

- ▶ To update a view, you may use the DROP statement and then the CREATE VIEW statement again.

Using Views to Simplify Complex Joins

One of the most common uses of views is to hide complex SQL, and this often involves joins. Look at the following statement:

Input ▼

```
CREATE VIEW productcustomers AS
SELECT cust_name, cust_contact, prod_id
FROM customers, orders, orderitems
WHERE customers.cust_id = orders.cust_id
  AND orderitems.order_num = orders.order_num;
```

Analysis ▼

This statement creates a view named productcustomers, which joins three tables to return a list of all customers who have ordered any product. If you were to SELECT * FROM productcustomers, you'd list every customer who ordered anything.

To retrieve a list of customers who ordered product TNT2, you can do the following:

Input ▼

```
SELECT cust_name, cust_contact
FROM productcustomers
WHERE prod_id = 'TNT2';
```

Output ▼

```
cust_nam                 cust_contact
--------------------     ------------
Coyote Inc.              Y Lee
Yosemite Place           Y Sam
```

Analysis ▼

This statement retrieves specific data from the view by issuing a WHERE clause. When SQL Server processes the request, it adds the specified WHERE clause to any existing WHERE clauses in the view query so the data is filtered correctly.

As you can see, views can greatly simplify the use of complex SQL statements. Using views, you can write the underlying SQL once and then reuse it as needed.

> **TIP: Creating Reusable Views**
>
> It is a good idea to create views that are not tied to specific data. For example, the view created in this example returns customers for all products, not just product TNT2 (for which the view was first created). Expanding the scope of the view enables it to be reused, making it even more useful. It also eliminates the need for you to create and maintain multiple similar views.

Using Views to Reformat Retrieved Data

As mentioned previously, another common use of views is for reformatting retrieved data. The following SELECT statement (from Lesson 9, "Creating Calculated Fields") returns vendor name and location in a single combined calculated column:

Input ▼

```
SELECT RTrim(vend_name) + ' (' + RTrim(vend_country) + ')'
       AS vend_title
FROM vendors
ORDER BY vend_name;
```

Output ▼

```
vend_title
--------------------------------------------------
ACME (USA)
Anvils R Us (USA)
Furball Inc. (USA)
Jet Set (England)
Jouets Et Ours (France)
LT Supplies (USA)
```

Now suppose that you regularly needed results in this format. Rather than perform the concatenation each time it is needed, you can create a view

and use that instead. To turn this statement into a view, you can do the
following:

Input ▼

```
CREATE VIEW vendorlocations AS
SELECT RTrim(vend_name) + ' (' + RTrim(vend_country) + ')'
       AS vend_title
FROM vendors;
```

Analysis ▼

This statement creates a view using the exact same query as the previous
SELECT statement. To retrieve the data to create all mailing labels, simply
do the following:

Input ▼

```
SELECT *
FROM vendorlocations
ORDER BY vend_title;
```

Output ▼

```
vend_title
- - - - - - - - - - - - - - - - - - - - - - - - - - - - - - - - - - - - - - - - - - - - - - - - - - -
ACME (USA)
Anvils R Us (USA)
Furball Inc. (USA)
Jet Set (England)
Jouets Et Ours (France)
LT Supplies (USA)
```

Using Views to Filter Unwanted Data

Views are also useful for applying common WHERE clauses. For example,
you might want to define a customeremaillist view that filters out customers without email addresses. To do this, you can use the following
statement:

Input ▼

```
CREATE VIEW customeremaillist AS
SELECT cust_id, cust_name, cust_email
FROM customers
WHERE cust_email IS NOT NULL;
```

Analysis ▼

Obviously, when sending email to a mailing list you'd want to ignore users who have no email address. The WHERE clause here filters out those rows that have NULL values in the cust_email columns so they'll not be retrieved.

View customeremaillist can now be used for data retrieval just like any table.

Input ▼

```
SELECT *
FROM customeremaillist;
```

Output ▼

```
cust_id      cust_name              cust_email
----------   --------------------   --------------------
10001        Coyote Inc.            ylee@coyote.com
10003        Wascals                rabbit@wascally.com
10004        Yosemite Place         sam@yosemite.com
10005        E Fudd                 elmer@fudd.com
```

> NOTE: WHERE **Clauses and** WHERE **Clauses**
> If you use a WHERE clause when retrieving data from the view, the two sets of clauses (the one in the view and the one passed to it) will be combined automatically.

Using Views with Calculated Fields

Views are exceptionally useful for simplifying the use of calculated fields. The following is a SELECT statement introduced in Lesson 9. It retrieves the order items for a specific order, calculating the expanded price for each item:

Input ▼

```
SELECT prod_id,
       quantity,
       item_price,
       quantity*item_price AS expanded_price
FROM orderitems
WHERE order_num = 20005;
```

Output ▼

prod_id	quantity	item_price	expanded_price
ANV01	10	5.99	59.90
ANV02	3	9.99	29.97
TNT2	5	10.00	50.00
FB	1	10.00	10.00

To turn this into a view, do the following:

Input ▼

```
CREATE VIEW orderitemsexpanded AS
SELECT order_num,
       prod_id,
       quantity,
       item_price,
       quantity*item_price AS expanded_price
FROM orderitems;
```

To retrieve the details for order 20005 (the previous output), do the following:

Input ▼

```
SELECT *
FROM orderitemsexpanded
WHERE order_num = 20005;
```

Output ▼

order_num	prod_id	quantity	item_price	expanded_price
20005	ANV01	10	5.99	59.90
20005	ANV02	3	9.99	29.97
20005	TNT2	5	10.00	50.00
20005	FB	1	10.00	10.00

As you can see, views are easy to create and even easier to use. Used correctly, views can greatly simplify complex data manipulation.

Updating Views

All of the views thus far have been used with SELECT statements. But can view data be updated? The answer is, it depends.

As a rule, yes, views are updateable (that is, you can use INSERT, UPDATE, and DELETE on them). Updating a view updates the underlying table (the view, you will recall, has no data of its own); if you add or remove rows from a view, you are actually adding them to or removing them from the underlying table.

But not all views are updateable. Basically, if SQL Server is unable to correctly ascertain the underlying data to be updated, updates (this includes inserts and deletes) are not allowed. In practice, this means that if any of the following are used, you'll not be able to update the view:

- ▶ Multiple base tables

- ▶ Grouping (using GROUP BY and HAVING)

- ▶ Joins

- ▶ Subqueries

- ▶ Unions

- ▶ Aggregate functions, such as Min(), Count(), Sum(), and so forth

- ▶ DISTINCT

- ▶ Derived (calculated) columns

In other words, many of the examples used in this lesson would not be updateable. This might sounds like a serious restriction, but in reality it isn't because views are primarily used for data retrieval anyway.

Summary

Views are virtual tables. They do not contain data; they contain queries that retrieve data, as needed, instead. Views provide a level of encapsulation around SQL Server SELECT statements and can be used to simplify data manipulation as well as to reformat or secure underlying data.

LESSON 22

Programming with T-SQL

Although T-SQL is not a general-purpose programming language, it does support programming constructs such as variables and conditional processing. Because these will be used in the next few lessons, this lesson introduces these T-SQL programming concepts.

Understanding T-SQL Programming

All of the SQL statements used thus far have been single standalone statements: SELECT statements to retrieve data, ALTER TABLE statements to make table changes, and so on. But some data-retrieval tasks are more complex, often involving multiple statements, conditional processing, and mid-process data manipulation.

T-SQL is not a general-purpose programming language, but it does support some basic programming ideas and constructs that can be used within data manipulation processes. These are generally not used when working with simple SQL statements, but are often used when working with stored procedures (introduced in Lesson 23, "Working with Stored Procedures"), cursors (see Lesson 24, "Using Cursors), triggers (explained in Lesson 25, "Using Triggers"), and more.

As such, it is worthwhile to briefly examine these capabilities, specifically the following:

- ▶ Using variables

- ▶ Performing conditional processing

- ▶ Repeating processes (looping)

Using Variables

In computer programming, a *variable* is a named object that stores values. Although variable use and capabilities vary from one programming language to the next, the basic ability to define variables and store values in them for subsequent use is pretty universal.

T-SQL variables have specific rules and requirements:

▶ All T-SQL variables names must start with @, local variables are prefixed with @, and global variables (which are used extensively by SQL Server itself and generally should not be used for your own purposes) are prefixed with @@.

▶ Before they can be used, T-SQL variables must be declared using the DECLARE statement.

▶ When a variable is declared, its datatype must be specified. (Refer to Lesson 1, "Understanding SQL," for an explanation of datatypes. In addition, Appendix D, "T-SQL Datatypes," lists the datatypes supported by SQL Server.)

▶ Multiple variables may be defined using individual DECLARE statements, or they may be comma-delimited in a single DECLARE statement.

▶ There is no way to "undeclare" variables. They remain present until they go out of scope. For local variables, this means they'll exist until the process completes.

Declaring Variables

The following example demonstrates the use of DECLARE:

Input ▼

```
DECLARE @age INT;
DECLARE @firstName CHAR(20), @lastName CHAR(20);
```

Analysis ▼

This example declares three variables. The first DECLARE statement declares a single variable named @age of type INT (an *integer*, a numeric value), and the second declares two variables of type CHAR(20) (a 20-character-length string). Notice that the second DECLARE statement requires a comma between the variables being declared.

Assigning Values to Variables

When variables are first declared, they contain no values (actually, they contain NULL). To assign values to variables, you use the SET statement, as shown here:

Input ▼

```
DECLARE @age INT;
DECLARE @firstName CHAR(20), @lastName CHAR(20);

SET @lastName='Forta';
SET @firstName='Ben';
SET @age=21;
```

Analysis ▼

This example declares the same three variables as seen previously, and then uses three SET statements to assign values to those variables (my name and age, wishfully thinking).

> TIP: **Assign Default Values**
> Many T-SQL developers find it useful to always initialize variables with default or initial values right after they have been declared.

You can also use SELECT to assign values to variables, as shown here:

Input ▼

```
SELECT @age=21;
```

In practice, SET is used to assign values to variables, unless the values are the result of a SELECT operation, in which case SELECT is obviously used.

> NOTE: SET **or** SELECT?
> There is one important difference between using SET or SELECT to assign variable values. SET only sets a single variable, and to assign values to multiple variables you must use multiple SET statements. SELECT, on the other hand, can be used to assign values to multiple variables in a single statement.

Viewing Variable Contents

When using variables, it is often necessary to inspect their contents. The simplest way to view variable contents is to output them, and there are two ways to do this. SELECT can be used to retrieve variable values, as shown here:

Input ▼

```
DECLARE @age INT;
DECLARE @firstName CHAR(20), @lastName CHAR(20);

SET @lastName='Forta';
SET @firstName='Ben';
SET @age=21;

SELECT @lastName, @firstName, @age
```

Output ▼

```
-------------------  -------------------  -----------
Forta                Ben                  21
```

Analysis ▼

As seen here, SELECT can return variables. However, the variable names themselves are not returned.

> **TIP: Use Aliases**
> You can use aliases in SELECT statements returning variables by using the AS keyword (see Lesson 9, "Creating Calculated Fields").

T-SQL also supports the PRINT statement, which is used to display messages along with any returned results. Here is an example:

Input ▼

```
DECLARE @age INT;
DECLARE @firstName CHAR(20), @lastName CHAR(20);

SET @lastName='Forta';
SET @firstName='Ben';
SET @age=21;

PRINT @lastName + ', ' + @firstName;
PRINT @age;
```

Output ▼

```
Forta          , Ben
21
```

Analysis ▼

PRINT simply outputs text. In this example, the first line is a string made up of three strings, a variable, static (fixed) text, and then another variable. The second line prints a numeric variable.

> **TIP: Converting Variables to Strings**
> What if you wanted to display the age output as Age: 21? You'd need to concatenate the string Age: with the variable @age, but the simple + concatenation operation used to join the strings together would fail because @age is a number, not a string. To get around this problem, you would need to convert @age to a string so as to be able to concatenate it, like this:
>
> ```
> PRINT 'Age: ' + Convert(CHAR, @age);
> ```

> NOTE: **Using the Debugger**
>
> There is another way to inspect variable contents. SQL Server supports the use of a debugger to step through SQL code line by line, allowing you to inspect variable contents in the process. Both SQL Server 2000 and SQL Server 2005 support debugger use, although the debuggers themselves (and how to use them) vary significantly between those two versions.
>
> Unfortunately, coverage of the SQL Server Debugger is beyond the scope of this book, but relevant documentation is included with SQL Server itself.

Using Variables in T-SQL Statements

Now that you know how to declare, populate, and view the contents of variables, let's look at a practical example of how variables could be used.

Suppose you need to run two queries, one to return customer information for a specific customer and another to return orders placed by that customer. This requires two SELECT statements, as shown here:

Input ▼

```
SELECT cust_name, cust_email
FROM customers
WHERE cust_id = 10001;

SELECT order_num, order_date
FROM orders
WHERE cust_id = 10001
ORDER BY order_date;
```

Output ▼

```
cust_name                           cust_email
-------------------------------     -------------------
Coyote Inc.                         ylee@coyote.com

order_num    order_date
----------   ------------------------
20005        2005-09-01 00:00:00.000
20009        2005-10-08 00:00:00.000
```

Analysis ▼

This batch-processing example is pretty self-explanatory; two SELECT statements are used, so two sets of results are returned.

> PLAIN ENGLISH: **Batch Processing**
>
> A *batch* is a set of SQL statements all submitted together to SQL Server for processing.

Notice that both SELECT statements use a cust_id value in their WHERE clauses. To run the same queries for another customer, you will need to update both WHERE clauses. Obviously, that leaves room for error; there is a possibility that someone will update one of the WHERE clauses but not the other, which would result in incorrect data being returned. In this simple example, there are only two places where the code would need updating to perform a different search. Imagine a more complex example, though, where the customer ID is used in lots of places. Obviously, the chance of error increases with the length and complexity of the code being used.

A better alternative to the preceding example would be to only define the customer ID once, thus only requiring one change to perform a different search. Look at this example:

Input ▼

```
-- Define @cust_id
DECLARE @cust_id INT;
SET @cust_id = 10001;

-- Get customer name and e-mail
SELECT cust_name, cust_email
FROM customers
WHERE cust_id = @cust_id;

-- Get customer order history
SELECT order_num, order_date
FROM orders
WHERE cust_id = @cust_id
ORDER BY order_date;
```

Output ▼

```
cust_name                         cust_email
-----------------------------     ------------------
Coyote Inc.                       ylee@coyote.com


order_num   order_date
-----------  -----------------------
20005        2005-09-01 00:00:00.000
20009        2005-10-08 00:00:00.000
```

Analysis ▼

In this example, the same two SELECT statements are used. But this time a local variable named @cust_id is first defined and populated. The two SELECT statements then use that variable in their WHERE clauses as WHERE cust_id = @cust_id. When processed by SQL Server, the value in the variable @cust_id will be used to construct the final WHERE clause.

CAUTION: **No Single Quotes when Using Variables**

As explained in Lesson 6, "Filtering Data," strings used in SQL statements are always enclosed within single quotes. But when using variables in a SQL statement, do not enclose single quotes around the variable names, even when using them as strings. Single quotes are needed when assigning values to string variables, but should not be used when you are actually using the variables.

TIP: **Comment Your Code**

You may have noticed that the preceding example contains lines of code beginning with - -. These are comments (messages included in your SQL code that are ignored by SQL Server), and they help explain what the code is doing. As the complexity of SQL statements increases, it is invaluable to be able to read embedded comments the next time someone has to understand what was done and why.

Using Conditional Processing

Conditional processing is a way to make decisions within programming code, performing some action based on the decision made. Like most other programming languages, T-SQL allows developers to write code where decisions are made at runtime, and what makes this work is the IF statement.

Let's start with a basic example. Imagine you are writing a SQL statement that has to process open orders (perhaps updating values, or copying rows to another table). This SQL code would need to run regularly, but what it does might differ based on whether today is a weekday (and thus a day when you are open for business and processing orders) or part of the weekend (when your are not processing orders).

Getting the current day of week is easy using T-SQL date and time functions (which were introduced back in Lesson 10, "Using Data Manipulation Functions"). GetDate() returns the current date and time, and DatePart() returns a part of a date (the day, the day of week, the month, and so on). To get the current day of week, you could use

```
DatePart(dw, GetDate())
```

The following is a simple IF statement that sets a variable to either 0 or 1, based on whether or not today is Sunday:

Input ▼

```
-- Define variables
DECLARE @open BIT

-- Open for business today?
IF DatePart(dw, GetDate()) = 1
    SET @open = 0
ELSE
    SET @open = 1

-- Output
SELECT @open AS OpenForBusiness
```

Output ▼

```
OpenForBusiness
---------------
1
```

Analysis ▼

Here, a local variable named @open is declared; it is of type BIT, which can only contain 0 (false, off, no) or 1 (true, on, yes). The IF statement compares the current day of week value, as returned by DatePart(dw, GetDate()), to 1 (Sunday), and sets @open to 0 if true (today is Sunday) or 1 if false (today is not Sunday). And then finally, @open is returned by a SELECT statement, although in reality @open would probably be used in subsequent processing (as opposed to simply being returned).

> NOTE: ELSE **Is Optional**
> The example here uses an ELSE clause to define the code to be processed if the IF test returns FALSE. The use of ELSE is optional, and many IF statements do not have an ELSE clause.

Of course, there is a flaw in this code because it only checks to see if today is Sunday. As such, if today were Saturday, @open would mistakenly be set to 1. To fix this we need to add an OR to the IF statement:

Input ▼

```
-- Define variables
DECLARE @dow INT
DECLARE @open BIT

-- Get the day of week
SET @dow = DatePart(dw, GetDate());

-- Open for business today?
IF @dow = 1 OR @dow = 7
    SET @open = 0
ELSE
    SET @open = 1

-- Output
SELECT @open AS OpenForBusiness
```

Analysis ▼

There are two changes in this version of the SQL code. An OR operator is now used in the IF statement so that either 1 (Sunday) or 7 (Saturday) match the test. In addition, instead of obtaining the current day of week right in the IF statement, we declare a local variable named @dow (for day of week) and populate it with the correct value. To understand the value of this change, look at the alternative:

```
IF DatePart(dw, GetDate()) = 1 OR DatePart(dw, GetDate()) = 7
```

So as to not have to obtain the current day of week twice in the IF statement, that code is processed earlier and the result is saved to a variable.

T-SQL supports both AND and OR operators in IF statements, as well as parentheses, which are used to define the order of evaluation. (Refer back to Lesson 7, "Advanced Data Filtering," for an introduction to AND, OR, and using parentheses to define the order of evaluation.)

Grouping Statements

As you have seen, IF is used to conditionally process whatever directly follows it. In the previous examples, a single statement was processed if the IF or ELSE conditions were met. But what would happen if you had to execute multiple statements? Look at this example:

Input ▼

```
-- Define variables
DECLARE @dow INT
DECLARE @open BIT, @process BIT

-- Get the day of week
SET @dow = DatePart(dw, GetDate());

-- Open for business today?
IF @dow = 1 OR @dow = 7
    SET @open = 0
    SET @process = 0
ELSE
    SET @open = 1
    SET @process = 1
```

Analysis ▼

If you were to run this code, an error would be generated. Why? Because once the IF has been processed, the first SET will either be processed (if the IF condition was met) or ignored (if the IF test failed). But regardless, the second SET statement will always be executed; it is not dependant on IF processing (even though the code indentation makes it appear to be). The error is actually caused by the ELSE statement, because SQL Server sees it as an extraneous ELSE not tied to any IF.

To solve this problem, two new keywords are needed, BEGIN and END. Look at this example:

Input ▼

```
-- Define variables
DECLARE @dow INT
DECLARE @open BIT, @process BIT

-- Get the day of week
SET @dow = DatePart(dw, GetDate());

-- Open for business today?
IF @dow = 1 OR @dow = 7
    BEGIN
        SET @open = 0
        SET @process = 0
    END
ELSE
    BEGIN
        SET @open = 1
        SET @process = 1
    END
```

Analysis ▼

Here, BEGIN and END are used to define a block of code. Now, when the IF or ELSE is processed, the entire block enclosed between BEGIN and END will be processed, instead of just the subsequent statement.

BEGIN and END are important statements, and are not just used in conjunction with IF, as will be shown in the upcoming lessons.

TIP: **Indent Your Code**

The code in the previous example uses two levels of indentation, the first to line up the code executed by IF or ELSE and the second to clearly define the contents of each BEGIN and END block. There are no hard-and-fast rules dictating how indentation is to be used; you can use the style used here, and anything else that helps you better organize and read your code.

Using Looping

SQL statements are processed sequentially, one at a time, and each being processed once. Like other programming languages, T-SQL supports looping, the ability to repeat a block of code as needed. In T-SQL, looping is accomplished using the WHILE statement.

NOTE: WHILE **and Cursors**

WHILE tends to be used most frequently in conjunction with cursors, as will be explained in Lesson 24.

The following is a simple (albeit atypical and rather useless) demonstration of how to use WHILE:

Input ▼

```
DECLARE @counter INT

SET @counter=1

WHILE @counter <= 10
BEGIN
    PRINT @counter
    SET @counter=@counter+1
END
```

Output ▼

```
1
2
3
4
5
6
7
8
9
10
```

Analysis ▼

This example defines a local variable named @counter and initializes it with a value of 1. The WHILE loop tests to see if @counter is less than or equal to 10, and as long as that condition is true, the number is displayed using PRINT and then incremented.

> NOTE: WHILE **and** BEGIN/END
>
> Just like IF, WHILE repeats only the single statement that follows it. To repeat multiple lines of code, use BEGIN and END to delimit that code block, as shown in the previous example.

Two other statements are frequently used in conjunction with WHILE:

▶ BREAK immediately exits the current WHILE loop (or IF).

▶ CONTINUE restarts processing at the top of the loop.

Summary

T-SQL supports basic programming constructs, including variables, conditional processing, and looping. In and of themselves, these are not that useful, but they are very important when used in conjunction with other SQL Server features, as you will see in the upcoming lessons.

Working with Stored Procedures

In this lesson, you'll learn what stored procedures are, why they are used, and how they are used. You'll also look at the basic syntax for creating and using them.

Understanding Stored Procedures

Most of the SQL statements that we've used thus far are simple in that they use a single statement against one or more tables. Not all operations are that simple; often, multiple statements will be needed to perform a complete operation. For example, consider the following scenario:

- ► To process an order, checks must be made to ensure that items are in stock.

- ► If items are in stock, they need to be reserved so they are not sold to anyone else, and the available quantity must be reduced to reflect the correct amount in stock.

- ► Any items not in stock need to be ordered; this requires some interaction with the vendor.

- ► The customer needs to be notified as to which items are in stock (and can be shipped immediately) and which are backordered.

This is obviously not a complete example, and it is even beyond the scope of the sample tables we have been using in this book, but it will suffice to help make a point. Performing this process requires many T-SQL statements against many tables. In addition, the exact statements that need to be performed and their order are not fixed; they can (and will) vary according to which items are in stock and which are not.

How would you write this code? You could write each of the statements individually and execute other statements conditionally, based on the result. You'd have to do this every time this processing was needed (and in every application that needed it).

Alternatively, you could create a stored procedure. Stored procedures are simply collections of one or more T-SQL statements saved for future use. You can think of them as batch files, although in truth they are more than that.

Why Use Stored Procedures

Now that you know what stored procedures are, why use them? There are many reasons, but here are the primary ones:

- ▶ To simplify complex operations (such as the previous example) by encapsulating processes into a single easy-to-use unit.

- ▶ To ensure data integrity by not requiring that a series of steps be created over and over. If all developers and applications use the same (tried-and-tested) stored procedure, the same code will be used by all.

  An extension of this is to prevent errors. The more steps that need to be performed, the more likely it is that errors will be introduced. Preventing errors ensures data consistency.

- ▶ To simplify change management. If tables, column names, or business logic (or just about anything) changes, only the stored procedure code needs to be updated, and no one else will need even to be aware that changes were made.

  An extension of this is security. Restricting access to underlying data via stored procedures reduces the chance of data corruption (unintentional or otherwise).

- To improve performance. Stored procedures typically execute quicker than individual SQL statements.

- Certain T-SQL language elements and SQL Server features are available only within single requests. Stored procedures can use these to create code that is more powerful and flexible. (You'll see an example of this in the next lesson.)

In other words, there are three primary benefits: simplicity, security, and performance. Obviously all are extremely important. Before you run off to turn all your SQL code into stored procedures, here's the downside:

- Stored procedures tend to be more complex to write than basic SQL statements, and writing them requires a greater degree of skill and experience.

- You might not have the security access needed to create stored procedures. Many database administrators restrict stored procedure–creation rights, allowing users to execute them but not necessarily create them.

Nonetheless, stored procedures are very useful and should be used whenever possible.

NOTE: Can't Write Them? You Can Still Use Them

SQL Server distinguishes the security and access needed to write stored procedures from the security and access needed to execute them. This is a good thing; even if you can't (or don't want to) write your own stored procedures, you can still execute them when appropriate.

Using Stored Procedures

Using stored procedures requires knowing how to execute (run) them. Stored procedures are executed far more often than they are written, so we'll start there. And then we'll look at creating and working with stored procedures.

Executing Stored Procedures

SQL Server procedures are executed using the EXECUTE statement. EXECUTE takes the name of the stored procedure and any parameters that need to be passed to it. Take a look at this example (you won't be able to actually run this one until we create it):

Input ▼

```
EXECUTE productpricing @cheap OUTPUT,
                       @expensive OUTPUT,
                       @average OUTPUT
```

Analysis ▼

Here, a stored procedure named productpricing is executed; it calculates and returns the lowest, highest, and average product prices into specified variables.

Stored procedures might or might not display results, as you will see shortly.

> TIP: EXECUTE **or** EXEC
>
> EXECUTE may be shortened to EXEC, but both EXECUTE and EXEC do the exact same thing.

Creating Stored Procedures

As already explained, writing a stored procedure is not trivial. To give you a taste for what is involved, let's look at a simple example, a stored procedure that returns the average product price. Here is the code:

Input ▼

```
CREATE PROCEDURE productpricing AS
BEGIN
    SELECT Avg(prod_price) AS priceaverage
    FROM products;
END;
```

Analysis ▼

The stored procedure is named `productpricing` and is thus defined with the statement `CREATE PROCEDURE productpricing AS`. The `BEGIN` and `END` statements are used to delimit the stored procedure body, and the body itself is just a simple `SELECT` statement, using the `Avg()` function you learned back in Lesson 11, "Summarizing Data."

When SQL Server processes this code, it creates a new stored procedure named `productpricing`. No data is returned because the code does not call the stored procedure; it simply creates the code for future use.

So how would you use this stored procedure? Like this:

Input ▼

```
EXECUTE productpricing;
```

Output ▼

```
priceaverage
--------------------
16.1335
```

Analysis ▼

`EXECUTE productpricing;` executes the just-created stored procedure and displays the returned result.

Dropping Stored Procedures

After they are created, stored procedures remain on the server, ready for use, until dropped. The `DROP` command (similar to the statement you saw in Lesson 20, "Creating and Manipulating Tables") removes the stored procedure from the server.

To remove the stored procedure we just created, use the following statement:

Input ▼

```
DROP PROCEDURE productpricing;
```

Analysis ▼

This drops (deletes) the just-created stored procedure.

Working with Parameters

productpricing is a really simple stored procedure; it simply displays the results of a SELECT statement. Typically stored procedures do not display results; rather, they return them to variables that you specify.

Here is an updated version of productpricing (you'll not be able to create the stored procedure again if you did not previously drop it):

Input ▼

```
CREATE PROCEDURE productpricing
    @price_min MONEY OUTPUT,
    @price_max MONEY OUTPUT,
    @price_avg MONEY OUTPUT

AS
BEGIN
    SELECT @price_min = Min(prod_price)
    FROM products;
    SELECT @price_max = Max(prod_price)
    FROM products;
    SELECT @price_avg = Avg(prod_price)
    FROM products;
END;
```

Analysis ▼

This stored procedure accepts three parameters: @price_min to store the lowest product price, @price_max to store the highest product price, and @price_avg to store the average product price. Each parameter must have its type specified (here, MONEY is used). The keyword OUTPUT is used to specify that this parameter is used to send a value out of the stored procedure (back to the caller). Without OUTPUT, the variables could only have been used to pass values to the stored procedure. The stored procedure code itself is enclosed within BEGIN and END statements, as shown before, and a series of SELECT statements are performed to retrieve the values that are then saved to the appropriate variables.

> **NOTE: Variables Must Start with @**
>
> As explained in Lesson 22, "Programming with T-SQL," all variable names must begin with @.

> **NOTE: Parameter Datatypes**
>
> The datatypes allowed in stored procedure parameters are the same as those used in tables. Appendix D, "T-SQL Datatypes," lists these types.

To call this updated stored procedure, we must specify three variable names, as shown here:

Input ▼

```
DECLARE @cheap MONEY
DECLARE @expensive MONEY
DECLARE @average MONEY

EXECUTE productpricing @cheap OUTPUT,
                       @expensive OUTPUT,
                       @average OUTPUT
```

Analysis ▼

Because the stored procedure expects three parameters, exactly three parameters must be passed, no more and no less. Therefore, three parameters are passed to this EXECUTE statement, and because variables are being used for the parameters, they must first be declared using DECLARE. These three variables are where the stored procedure will return results, so each must be passed as OUTPUT (or values will not be returned in them). These variables need not be named the same as the receiving variables within the stored procedure itself, and indeed they are not in this example.

When called, this statement does not actually display any data. Rather, it returns variables that can then be displayed (or used in other processing).

To display the retrieved average product price, you could do the following:

Input ▼

```
SELECT @cheap;
```

Output ▼

```
Cheap
--------------------
2.50
```

To obtain all three values, you can use the following:

Input ▼

```
SELECT @cheap, @expensive, @average;
```

Output ▼

```
Cheap    Expensive  Average
-------  ---------  -------
2.50     55.00      16.1335
```

Here is another example. This time the example passes parameters to the stored procedure as well as returns OUTPUT parameters. ordertotal accepts an order number and returns the total for that order:

Input ▼

```
CREATE PROCEDURE ordertotal
    @order_num INT,
    @order_total MONEY OUTPUT

AS
BEGIN
   SELECT @order_total = Sum(item_price*quantity)
   FROM orderitems
   WHERE order_num = @order_num;
END;
```

Analysis ▼

@order_num is used to pass a value to the stored procedure, so OUTPUT is not needed. @order_total is defined as OUTPUT because the total is to be returned from the stored procedure. The SELECT statement uses both of these parameters, the WHERE clause uses @order_num to select the right rows, and @order_total stores the calculated total.

To invoke this new stored procedure, you can use the following:

Input ▼

```
DECLARE @order_total MONEY
EXECUTE ordertotal 20005, @order_total OUTPUT
SELECT @order_total
```

Output ▼

```
- - - - - - - - - - - - - - - - - - - -
149.87
```

Analysis ▼

Two parameters must be passed to ordertotal; the first is the order number and the second is the name of the variable that will contain the calculated total. Here, one of those parameters (the order number) is a static value (not a variable).

To obtain a display for the total of another order, you would need to call the stored procedure again and then redisplay the variable:

Input ▼

```
DECLARE @order_total MONEY
EXECUTE ordertotal 20009, @order_total OUTPUT
SELECT @order_total
```

Building Intelligent Stored Procedures

All of the stored procedures used thus far have basically encapsulated simple T-SQL SELECT statements. And although they are all valid examples of stored procedures, they really don't do anything more than what you could do with those statements directly (if anything, they just make things a little more complex). The real power of stored procedures is realized when business rules and intelligent processing are included within them.

Consider this scenario: You need to obtain order totals as before, but also need to add sales tax to the total, but only for some customers (perhaps the ones in your own state). Now you need to do several things:

▶ Obtain the total (as before).

▶ Conditionally add tax to the total.

▶ Return the total (with or without tax).

That's a perfect job for a stored procedure:

Input ▼

```
-- Name: ordertotal
-- Parameters: @order_num   = order number
--             @taxable     = 0 if not taxable, 1 if taxable
--             @order_total = order total variable

CREATE PROCEDURE ordertotal
    @order_num INT,
    @taxable BIT,
    @order_total MONEY OUTPUT
AS
BEGIN

    -- Declare variable for total
    DECLARE @total MONEY;
    -- Declare tax percentage
    DECLARE @taxrate INT;
    -- Set tax rate (adjust as needed)
    SET @taxrate = 6;

    -- Get the order total
    SELECT @total = Sum(item_price*quantity)
    FROM orderitems
    WHERE order_num = @order_num
```

```
-- Is this taxable?
IF @taxable = 1
   -- Yes, so add taxrate to the total
   SET @total=@total+(@total/100*@taxrate);

   -- And finally, save to output variable
   SELECT @order_total = @total;

END;
```

> **TIP: First DROP If Needed**
> You may need to DROP the existing stored procedure before you can save this new version.

Analysis ▼

The stored procedure has changed dramatically. First of all, comments have been added throughout (preceded by -- , as explained in Lesson 22). An additional parameter has been added, @taxable of type BIT (which specifies 1 if taxable, 0 if not). Within the stored procedure body, two local variables are defined using DECLARE statements, and @taxrate in this example is set to 6%. The SELECT has changed, so the result is stored in @total (a local variable) instead of @order_total. Then an IF statement checks to see if @taxable is true, and if it is, a SET statement is used to add the tax to local variable @total. And finally, @total (which might or might not have had tax added) is saved to @order_total using another SELECT statement.

This is obviously a more sophisticated and powerful stored procedure. To try it out, use the following two statements:

Input ▼

```
DECLARE @order_total MONEY
EXECUTE ordertotal 20005, 0, @order_total OUTPUT
SELECT @order_total
```

Output ▼

```
149.87
```

Input ▼

```
DECLARE @order_total MONEY
EXECUTE ordertotal 20005, 1, @order_total OUTPUT
SELECT @order_total
```

Output ▼

```
158.8622
```

Analysis ▼

The only difference between the two EXECUTE calls is the second parameter: 0 (false) is passed for the first, and 1 (true) is passed for the second. This makes it easy to conditionally add tax to the order total.

Summary

In this lesson, you learned what stored procedures are and why they are used. You also learned the basics of stored procedure execution and creation syntax, and you saw some of the ways these can be used. Stored procedures are often used in conjunction with cursor operations, and so we'll look at cursors in the next lesson.

LESSON 24

Using Cursors

In this lesson, you'll learn what cursors are and how to use them.

Understanding Cursors

As you have seen in previous lessons, T-SQL retrieval operations work with sets of rows known as *result sets*. The rows returned are all the rows that match a SQL statement, zero or more of them. Using simple SELECT statements, there is no way to get the first row, the next row, or the previous 10 rows, for example. Nor is there an easy way to process all rows, one at a time (as opposed to all of them in a batch).

Sometimes there is a need to step through rows forward or backward, and one or more at a time. This is what cursors are used for. A cursor is a database query stored in SQL Server, not a SELECT statement, but the result set retrieved by that statement. Once the cursor is stored, applications can scroll or browse up and down through the data as needed.

Cursors are used primarily by interactive applications in which users need to scroll up and down through screens of data, browsing or making changes.

Working with Cursors

Using cursors involves several distinct steps:

1. Before a cursor can be used, it must be declared (defined). This process does not actually retrieve any data; it merely defines the SELECT statement to be used.

2. After it is declared, the cursor must be opened for use. This process actually retrieves the data using the previously defined SELECT statement.

3. With the cursor populated with data, individual rows can be fetched (retrieved) as needed.

4. Once the desired data has been fetched, the cursor must be closed.

5. Finally, the cursor must be removed.

After a cursor is declared, it may be opened and closed as often as needed (until it is removed). After the cursor is open, fetch operations can be performed as often as needed.

Creating and Removing Cursors

Cursors are created using the DECLARE statement (discussed in Lesson 22, "Programming with T-SQL"). DECLARE names the cursor and takes a SELECT statement, complete with WHERE and other clauses if needed. When a cursor is no longer needed, it must be removed using DEALLOCATE.

> NOTE: **Implicit** DEALLOCATE
>
> DEALLOCATE can actually be omitted, in which case SQL Server will automatically remove the cursor when it goes out of scope.

For example, this statement defines a cursor named orders_cursor using a SELECT statement that retrieves all order numbers:

Input ▼

```
DECLARE orders_cursor CURSOR
FOR
SELECT order_num FROM orders ORDER BY order_num;

DEALLOCATE orders_cursor;
```

Analysis ▼

A DECLARE statement is used to define and name the cursor, in this case, orders_cursor. Nothing is done with the cursor, and it is immediately removed using DEALLOCATE.

> **NOTE: Can Only DECLARE Once**
> Once a cursor has been declared, it cannot be declared again, even if the DECLARE statement is identical to the one used previously. To change a cursor, you must first remove it with DEALLOCATE and then declare it again with DECLARE.

Now that the cursor is defined, it is ready to be opened.

Opening and Closing Cursors

Cursors are opened using the OPEN statement, like this:

Input ▼

```
OPEN orders_cursor;
```

Analysis ▼

When the OPEN statement is processed, the query is executed, and the retrieved data is stored for subsequent browsing and scrolling.

After cursor processing is complete, the cursor should be closed using the CLOSE statement, as follows:

Input ▼

```
CLOSE orders_cursor;
```

Analysis ▼

CLOSE frees up internal memory and resources used by the cursor, so every cursor should be closed when it is no longer needed.

After a cursor is closed, it cannot be reused without being opened again. However, a cursor does not need to be declared again to be used; an OPEN statement is sufficient (so long as the cursor has not been removed with DEALLOCATE).

Here is an updated version of the previous example:

Input ▼

```
-- Define the cursor
DECLARE orders_cursor CURSOR
FOR
SELECT order_num FROM orders ORDER BY order_num;

-- Open cursor (retrieve data)
OPEN orders_cursor;

-- Close cursor
CLOSE orders_cursor

-- And finally, remove it
DEALLOCATE orders_cursor;
```

Analysis ▼

This stored procedure declares, opens, closes, and then removes a cursor. However, nothing is done with the retrieved data.

Using Cursor Data

After a cursor is opened, you can access each row individually using a FETCH statement. FETCH specifies the cursor to be used and where retrieved data should be stored. It also advances the internal row pointer within the cursor so the next FETCH statement will retrieve the next row (and not the same one over and over).

The first example retrieves a single row from the cursor (the first row):

Input ▼

```
-- Local variables
DECLARE @order_num INT;

-- Define the cursor
DECLARE orders_cursor CURSOR
FOR
SELECT order_num FROM orders ORDER BY order_num;

-- Open cursor (retrieve data)
OPEN orders_cursor;

-- Perform the first fetch (get first row)
FETCH NEXT FROM orders_cursor INTO @order_num;

-- Close cursor
CLOSE orders_cursor

-- And finally, remove it
DEALLOCATE orders_cursor;
```

Analysis ▼

Here, FETCH is used to retrieve the order_num column of the current row (it'll start at the first row automatically) and place it into a local declared variable named @order_num. Nothing is done with the retrieved data.

> **NOTE: What to Fetch?**
>
> The FETCH statements in this example use FETCH NEXT to fetch the next row. This is the most frequently used FETCH, but other FETCH options are available. These include FETCH PRIOR to retrieve the previous row, FETCH FIRST and FETCH LAST to retrieve the first and last rows, respectively, FETCH ABSOLUTE to fetch a specific row number starting from the top, and FETCH RELATIVE to fetch a specific row number starting from the current row.

In the next example, the retrieved data is looped through from the first row to the last:

Input ▼

```
-- Local variables
DECLARE @order_num INT;

-- Define the cursor
DECLARE orders_cursor CURSOR
FOR
SELECT order_num FROM orders ORDER BY order_num;

-- Open cursor (retrieve data)
OPEN orders_cursor;

-- Perform the first fetch (get first row)
FETCH NEXT FROM orders_cursor INTO @order_num;

-- Check @@FETCH_STATUS to see if there are any more rows
-- to fetch.
WHILE @@FETCH_STATUS = 0
BEGIN
    -- This is executed as long as the previous fetch succeeds.
    FETCH NEXT FROM orders_cursor INTO @order_num;
END

-- Close cursor
CLOSE orders_cursor

-- And finally, remove it
DEALLOCATE orders_cursor;
```

Analysis ▼

Like the previous example, this code uses FETCH to retrieve the current order_num and place it into a declared variable named @order_num. Unlike the previous example, the FETCH here is followed by a WHILE loop, so it is repeated over and over. When does the looping terminate? Each time FETCH is used, an internal function named @@FETCH_STATUS obtains a status code. @@FETCH_STATUS will return 0 if the FETCH succeeded, and a negative value otherwise. So the WHILE loop simply continues WHILE @@FETCH_STATUS = 0.

With this functionality in place, you can now place any needed processing inside the loop (after the BEGIN statement and before the next FETCH).

To put this all together, here is one further revision of our sample cursor, this time with some actual processing of fetched data:

Input ▼

```
-- Local variables
DECLARE @order_num INT;
DECLARE @order_total MONEY;
DECLARE @total MONEY;

-- Initialize @total
SET @total=0;

-- Define the cursor
DECLARE orders_cursor CURSOR
FOR
SELECT order_num FROM orders ORDER BY order_num;

-- Open cursor (retrieve data)
OPEN orders_cursor;

-- Perform the first fetch (get first row)
FETCH NEXT FROM orders_cursor INTO @order_num;

-- Check @@FETCH_STATUS to see if there are any more rows
-- to fetch.
WHILE @@FETCH_STATUS = 0
BEGIN
    -- Get this order total (including tax)
    EXECUTE ordertotal @order_num, 1, @order_total OUTPUT

    -- Add this order to the total
    SET @total = @total + @order_total

    -- Get next row
    FETCH NEXT FROM orders_cursor INTO @order_num;
END

-- Close cursor
CLOSE orders_cursor
```

```
-- And finally, remove it
DEALLOCATE orders_cursor;

-- And finally display calculated total
SELECT @total AS GrantTotal;
```

Analysis ▼

In this example, we've declared a variable named `@order_total` (to store the total for each order) and another named `@total` (to store the running total of all orders). `FETCH` fetches each `@order_num` as it did before, and then `EXECUTE` is used to execute a stored procedure (the one we created in the previous lesson) to calculate the total with tax for each order (the result of which is stored in `@order_total`). Each time an `@order_total` is retrieved, it is added to `@total` using a `SET` statement. And finally, the grant total is returned using a `SELECT`.

And there you have it, a complete working example of cursors, row-by-row processing, and even stored procedures execution.

Summary

In this lesson, you learned what cursors are and why they are used. You also saw examples demonstrating basic cursor use, as well as techniques for looping through cursor results and for row-by-row processing.

LESSON 25

Using Triggers

In this lesson, you'll learn what triggers are, why they are used, and how. You'll also look at the syntax for creating and using them.

Understanding Triggers

T-SQL statements are executed when needed, as are stored procedures. But what if you want a statement (or statements) to be executed automatically when events occur? Here are some examples:

- ▶ Every time a customer is added to a database table, check that the phone number is formatted correctly and that the state abbreviation is in uppercase.

- ▶ Every time a product is ordered, subtract the ordered quantity from the number in stock.

- ▶ Whenever a row is deleted, save a copy in an archive table.

What all these examples have in common is that they need to be processed automatically whenever a table change occurs. And that is exactly what triggers are. A *trigger* is a T-SQL statement (or a group of statements enclosed within BEGIN and END statements) that is automatically executed by SQL Server in response to any of these statements:

- ▶ DELETE

- ▶ INSERT

- ▶ UPDATE

No other T-SQL statements support triggers.

> NOTE: **Tables and Views**
> Triggers are supported on tables and views (but not on temporary tables).

Creating Triggers

When creating a trigger, you need to specify three pieces of information:

- ▶ The unique trigger name

- ▶ The table to which the trigger is to be associated

- ▶ The action that the trigger should respond to (DELETE, INSERT, or UPDATE)

Triggers are created using the CREATE TRIGGER statement. Here is a really simple example:

Input ▼

```
CREATE TRIGGER newproduct_trigger ON products
AFTER INSERT
AS
SELECT 'Product added';
```

Analysis ▼

CREATE TRIGGER is used to create the new trigger named newproduct_ trigger. This trigger is defined as AFTER INSERT, so the trigger will execute after a successful INSERT statement has been executed, and the text Product added will be displayed once for each row inserted.

To test this trigger, use the INSERT statement to add one or more rows to products; you'll see the Product added message displayed for each successful insertion.

Triggers are defined per event per table, and only one trigger per event per table is allowed. As such, up to three triggers are supported per table (one for each of INSERT, UPDATE, and DELETE).

> TIP: **Multiple Events per Trigger**
> A single trigger can be associated with multiple events, so if you need a trigger to be executed for both INSERT and UPDATE operations, you can define it as AFTER INSERT, UPDATE.

> NOTE: INSTEAD OF **Triggers**
> Most triggers are AFTER triggers; they are executed after an event occurs. SQL Server supports another type of trigger called an INSTEAD OF trigger, which, if defined, is invoked instead of the original T-SQL statement. For example, if you want to never allow rows to be deleted, you could create an INSTEAD OF trigger that replaces DELETE on a specific table with a T-SQL statement that updates the rows to make them inactive (perhaps by setting a flag in those rows). INSTEAD OF triggers are not covered in this lesson.

Dropping Triggers

By now the syntax for dropping a trigger should be self-apparent. To drop a trigger, use the DROP TRIGGER statement, as shown here:

Input ▼

```
DROP TRIGGER newproduct_trigger;
```

Analysis ▼

This example removes trigger newproduct_trigger.

> TIP: **Updating Triggers**
> Triggers can be updated using ALTER TRIGGER, or they can be dropped and re-created.

Enabling and Disabling Triggers

It is sometimes necessary to be able to execute T-SQL statements without executing defined triggers. Rather than dropping the triggers and then having to re-create them, SQL Server allows you to disable triggers and then enable them as needed.

To disable a trigger, use the DISABLE TRIGGER statement, as shown here:

Input ▼

```
DISABLE TRIGGER newproduct_trigger ON products;
```

To reenable a trigger, use the ENABLE TRIGGER statement, as shown here:

Input ▼

```
ENABLE TRIGGER newproduct_trigger ON products;
```

Determining Trigger Assignments

Triggers are very useful and very powerful. But they can also change the way SQL Server behaves, executing code that you may be unaware of. And because most triggers execute silently (they provide no feedback), it can be difficult to determine whether triggers are running at any given time.

To solve this problem, you can use the built-in stored procedure SP_HELPTRIGGER:

Input ▼

```
SP_HELPTRIGGER products;
```

Analysis ▼

SP_HELPTRIGGER takes the name of a table and returns a list of triggers (if any are defined), with flags indicating the trigger type. If you were to run this code after creating the newproduct trigger discussed above, ISINSERT and ISAFTER would both be 1 because we created that trigger AFTER INSERT.

Using Triggers

With the basics covered, we will now look at each of the supported trigger types and the differences between them.

INSERT Triggers

INSERT triggers are executed after an INSERT statement is executed. Within INSERT trigger code, you can refer to a virtual table named INSERTED to access the rows being inserted.

Here's an example (a really useful one, actually). IDENTITY columns have values that are automatically assigned by SQL Server. Lesson 20, "Creating and Manipulating Tables," suggested several ways to determine the newly generated value, but here is an even better solution:

Input ▼

```
CREATE TRIGGER neworder_trigger ON orders
AFTER INSERT
AS
SELECT @@IDENTITY AS order_num;
```

Analysis ▼

The code creates a trigger named neworder_trigger that is executed AFTER INSERT on the table orders. When a new order is saved in orders, SQL Server generates a new order number and saves it in order_num. This trigger simply obtains this value from @@IDENTITY and returns it. Using this trigger for every insertion into orders will always return the new order number.

To test this trigger, try inserting a new order, like this:

Input ▼

```
INSERT INTO orders(order_date, cust_id)
VALUES(GetDate(), 10001);
```

Output ▼

```
order_num
------------
20010
```

Analysis ▼

orders contains three columns. order_date and cust_id must be specified, order_num is automatically generated by SQL Server, and order_num
is now returned automatically.

DELETE Triggers

DELETE triggers are executed after a DELETE statement is executed. Within
DELETE trigger code, you can refer to a virtual table named DELETED to
access the rows being deleted.

The following example demonstrates the use of DELETED to save deleted
rows into an archive table:

Input ▼

```
CREATE TRIGGER deleteorder_trigger ON orders
AFTER DELETE
AS
BEGIN
    INSERT INTO orders_archive(order_num, order_date, cust_id)
    SELECT order_num, order_date, cust_id FROM DELETED;
END;
```

Analysis ▼

This trigger is executed when rows are deleted from the orders table. It
uses an INSERT SELECT statement to save the rows in DELETE into an
archive table named orders_archive. (To actually use this example,
you'll need to create a table named orders_archive with the same
columns as orders.)

> **NOTE: Multistatement Triggers**
> You'll notice that trigger deleteorder_trigger uses BEGIN and END statements to mark the trigger body. This is actually not necessary in this example, although it does no harm being there. The advantage of using a BEGIN END block is that the trigger would then be able to accommodate multiple SQL statements (one after the other within the BEGIN END block). BEGIN END was introduced in Lesson 22, "Programming with T-SQL."

UPDATE Triggers

UPDATE triggers are executed after an UPDATE statement is executed. Within UPDATE trigger code, you can refer to a virtual table named DELETED to access the previous (pre-UPDATE statement) values and INSERTED to access the new updated values.

The following example ensures that state abbreviations are always in uppercase (regardless of how they were actually specified in the UPDATE statement):

Input ▼

```
CREATE TRIGGER vendor_trigger ON vendors
AFTER INSERT, UPDATE
AS
BEGIN
    UPDATE vendors
    SET vend_state=Upper(vend_state)
    WHERE vend_id IN (SELECT vend_id FROM INSERTED);
END;
```

Analysis ▼

This trigger is executed AFTER INSERT, UPDATE. Each time rows are inserted or updated, the values in vend_state are replaced with Upper(vend_state).

More on Triggers

Before we wrap up this lesson, here are some important points to keep in mind when using triggers:

- ▸ Creating triggers might require special security access. However, trigger execution is automatic. If an INSERT, UPDATE, or DELETE statement may be executed, any associated triggers will be executed, too.

- ▸ Triggers should be used to ensure data consistency (case, formatting, and so on). The advantage of performing this type of processing in a trigger is that it always happens, and happens transparently, regardless of client application.

- ▸ One very interesting use for triggers is in creating an audit trail. Using triggers, it would be very easy to log changes (even before and after states if needed) to another table.

- ▸ Triggers can call stored procedures as well as most T-SQL statements.

Summary

In this lesson, you learned what triggers are and why they are used. You also saw examples of triggers used for INSERT, DELETE, and UPDATE operations.

LESSON 26

Managing Transaction Processing

In this lesson, you'll learn what transactions are and how to use COMMIT *and* ROLLBACK *statements to manage transaction processing.*

Understanding Transaction Processing

Transaction processing is used to maintain database integrity by ensuring that batches of T-SQL operations execute completely or not at all.

As explained back in Lesson 14, "Joining Tables," relational databases are designed so data is stored in multiple tables to facilitate easier data manipulation, management, and reuse. Without going into the how and why of relational database design, take it as a given that well-designed database schemas are relational to some degree.

The orders tables you've been using in prior lessons are a good example of this. Orders are stored in two tables: orders stores actual orders, and orderitems stores the individual items ordered. These two tables are related to each other using unique IDs called *primary keys* (as discussed in Lesson 1, "Understanding SQL"). These tables, in turn, are related to other tables containing customer and product information.

The process of adding an order to the system is as follows:

1. Check whether the customer is already in the database (present in the customers table). If not, add him or her.

2. Retrieve the customer's ID.

3. Add a row to the orders table associating it with the customer ID.

4. Retrieve the new order ID assigned in the orders table.

5. Add one row to the orderitems table for each item ordered, associating it with the orders table by the retrieved ID (and with the products table by product ID).

Now imagine that some database failure (for example, out of disk space, security restrictions, table locks) prevents this entire sequence from completing. What would happen to your data?

Well, if the failure occurred after the customer was added and before the orders table was added, there is no real problem. It is perfectly valid to have customers without orders. When you run the sequence again, the inserted customer record will be retrieved and used. You can effectively pick up where you left off.

But what if the failure occurred after the orders row was added, but before the orderitems rows were added? Now you'd have an empty order sitting in your database.

Worse, what if the system failed during adding the orderitems rows? Now you'd end up with a partial order in your database, but you wouldn't know it.

How do you solve this problem? That's where transaction processing comes in. *Transaction processing* is a mechanism used to manage sets of T-SQL operations that must be executed in batches to ensure that databases never contain the results of partial operations. With transaction processing, you can ensure that sets of operations are not aborted mid-processing; they either execute in their entirety or not at all (unless explicitly instructed otherwise). If no error occurs, the entire set of statements is committed (written) to the database tables. If an error does occur, a rollback (undo) can occur to restore the database to a known and safe state.

So, looking at the same example, this is how the process would work:

1. Check whether the customer is already in the database; if not, add him or her.

2. Commit the customer information.

3. Retrieve the customer's ID.

4. Add a row to the orders table.

5. If a failure occurs while adding the row to orders, roll back.

6. Retrieve the new order ID assigned in the orders table.

7. Add one row to the orderitems table for each item ordered.

8. If a failure occurs while adding rows to orderitems, roll back all the orderitems rows added and the orders row.

9. Commit the order information.

When working with transactions and transaction processing, you'll notice a few keywords that keep reappearing. Here are the terms you need to know:

▶ **Transaction:** A block of SQL statements

▶ **Rollback:** The process of undoing specified SQL statements

▶ **Commit:** Writing unsaved SQL statements to the database tables

▶ **Savepoint:** A temporary placeholder in a transaction set to which you can issue a rollback (as opposed to rolling back an entire transaction)

Controlling Transactions

Now that you know what transaction processing is, let's look at what is involved in managing transactions.

The key to managing transactions involves breaking your SQL statements into logical chunks and explicitly stating when data should be rolled back and when it should not.

The T-SQL statement used to mark the start of a transaction is

Input ▼

```
BEGIN TRANSACTION;
```

Transactions may optionally be named. This is useful when you are working with multiple transactions so as to be able to explicitly define the transaction to be committed if rolled back.

Using ROLLBACK

The T-SQL ROLLBACK command is used to roll back (undo) T-SQL statements, as shown in this next statement (feel free to try this one, and yes, I know the code is scary):

Input ▼

```
-- What is in orderitems?
SELECT * FROM orderitems;
-- Start the transaction
BEGIN TRANSACTION;
-- Delete all rows from orderitems
DELETE FROM orderitems;
-- Verify that they are gone
SELECT * FROM orderitems;
-- Now rollback the transaction
ROLLBACK;
-- And the deleted rows should all be back
SELECT * FROM orderitems;
```

Analysis ▼

This example starts by displaying the contents of the orderitems table. First, a SELECT is performed to show that the table is not empty. Then a transaction is started, and all of the rows in orderitems are deleted with a DELETE statement. Another SELECT verifies that, indeed, orderitems is empty. Then a ROLLBACK statement is used to roll back all statements until the BEGIN TRANSACTION, and the final SELECT shows that the table is no longer empty.

Obviously, ROLLBACK can only be used within a transaction (after a BEGIN TRANSACTION command has been issued).

> TIP: **Which Statements Can You Roll Back?**
> Transaction processing is used to manage INSERT, UPDATE, and DELETE statements. You cannot roll back SELECT statements. (There would not be much point in doing so anyway.) You cannot roll back CREATE and DROP operations. These statements may be used in a transaction block, but if you perform a rollback, they will not be undone.

Using COMMIT

T-SQL statements are usually executed and written directly to the database tables. This is known as an *autocommit*; the commit (write or save) operation happens automatically.

Within a transaction block, however, commits do not occur implicitly. To force an explicit commit, you use the COMMIT statement, as shown here:

Input ▼

```
BEGIN TRANSACTION;
DELETE FROM orderitems WHERE order_num = 20010;
DELETE FROM orders WHERE order_num = 20010;
COMMIT;
```

Analysis ▼

In this example, order number 20010 is deleted entirely from the system. Because this involves updating two database tables, orders and orderitems, a transaction block is used to ensure that the order is not partially deleted. The final COMMIT statement writes the change only if no error occurred. If the first DELETE worked, but the second failed, the DELETE would not be committed. (It would effectively be automatically undone.)

This example uses a single COMMIT at the ends of the statement batch.

More complex examples often use multiple ROLLBACK and COMMIT statements to write changes whenever needed (and only when wanted).

NOTE: **Implicit Transaction Closes**
After a COMMIT or ROLLBACK statement has been executed, the transaction is automatically closed (and future changes will implicitly commit).

Using Savepoints

Simple ROLLBACK and COMMIT statements enable you to write or undo an entire transaction. Although this works for simple transactions, more complex transactions might require partial commits or rollbacks.

For example, the process of adding an order described previously is a single transaction. If an error occurs, you only want to roll back to the point before the orders row was added. You do not want to roll back the addition to the customers table (if there was one).

To support the rollback of partial transactions, you must be able to put placeholders at strategic locations in the transaction block. Then, if a rollback is required, you can roll back to one of the placeholders.

These placeholders are called *savepoints*, and to create one use the SAVE TRANSACTION statement, as follows:

Input ▼

```
SAVE TRANSACTION delete1;
```

NOTE: **Savepoint Names**
Generally, each savepoint should a unique name that identifies it so that, when you roll back, SQL Server knows where you are rolling back to. In practice, however, savepoint names may be reused, in which case SQL Server will roll back to the most recent savepoint of that name.

To roll back to this savepoint, do the following:

Input ▼

```
ROLLBACK TRANSACTION delete1;
```

To roll back to the very beginning of the transaction, do the following:

Input ▼

```
ROLLBACK TRANSACTION;
```

TIP: **The More Savepoints the Better**
You can have as many savepoints as you'd like within your T-SQL code, and the more the better. Why? Because the more savepoints you have, the more flexibility you have in managing rollbacks exactly as you need them.

Changing Autocommit Behavior

As already explained, the default SQL Server behavior is to automatically commit any and all changes. In other words, any time you execute a T-SQL statement, that statement is actually being performed against the tables, and the changes made occur immediately. To instruct SQL Server to not automatically commit changes, you need to use the following statement:

Input ▼

```
SET IMPLICIT_TRANSACTIONS ON;
```

Analysis ▼

The IMPLICIT_TRANSACTIONS setting determines whether changes are committed automatically without requiring a manual COMMIT statement. Setting IMPLICIT_TRANSACTIONS to ON instructs SQL Server to not automatically commit changes (until the flag is set back to OFF).

Summary

In this lesson, you learned that transactions are blocks of SQL statements that must be executed as a batch. You learned how to use the COMMIT and ROLLBACK statements to explicitly manage when data is written and when it is undone. You also learned how to use savepoints to provide a greater level of control over rollback operations.

LESSON 27

Working with XML

In this lesson, you'll learn how to generate well-formed XML from relational data. You will also learn about the XML datatype and how it is used.

Understanding SQL Server XML Support

> NOTE: **SQL Server 2005 Only**
> This lesson covers functionality that was introduced in SQL Server 2005 and is not available in earlier versions of SQL Server.

XML has become a standard mechanism by which to exchange, distribute, and persist data. Although SQL Server is a relational DBMS, and relational data is very different from hierarchical XML data, there are often compelling reasons to obtain SQL Server data as XML, and to store XML data within SQL Server tables.

Here are the three primary areas of interest concerning SQL Server's XML support:

- ► Using SELECT to retrieve data, returning it as well-formed XML.
- ► Storing well-formed XML within specific columns in database tables.
- ► Being able to search for data based on content within specific XML elements.

> NOTE: **Just the Basics**
> This lesson does not attempt to teach XML itself. XML (including the use of XPath to work with XML data, and XQuery to search XML data) is a broad topic, and is the subject of many books. If you need to work with XML data, you should definitely take the time to better understand XML data structures and how to work with them.

Retrieving Data as XML

Relational data stored in SQL Server tables can be retrieved as well-formed XML, ready for consumption by an XML client or application of your choice. To retrieve data as XML, use SELECT with an added FOR XML clause.

Here is a simple example:

Input ▼

```
SELECT vend_id, RTrim(vend_name) AS vend_name
FROM vendors
ORDER BY vend_name
FOR XML AUTO;
```

Output ▼

```
<vendors vend_id="1003" vend_name="ACME" />
<vendors vend_id="1001" vend_name="Anvils R Us" />
<vendors vend_id="1004" vend_name="Furball Inc." />
<vendors vend_id="1005" vend_name="Jet Set" />
<vendors vend_id="1006" vend_name="Jouets Et Ours" />
<vendors vend_id="1002" vend_name="LT Supplies" />
```

Analysis ▼

FOR XML instructs SQL Server to generate XML output. When generating XML, you'd usually need to define the shape of the desired XML, but AUTO simplifies that by creating output based on the columns and order used. Here, each vendor is listed as a separate XML element, the table name vendors is used as the element name, and the two selected columns are used as attributes.

Here is a slightly more complex example:

Input ▼

```
SELECT cust_name, orders.order_num, products.prod_id,
       prod_name
FROM customers, orders, orderitems, products
WHERE customers.cust_id=orders.cust_id
 AND orders.order_num=orderitems.order_num
 AND orderitems.prod_id=products.prod_id
ORDER BY cust_name, orders.order_num, products.prod_id
FOR XML AUTO;
```

Output ▼

```
<customers cust_name="Coyote Inc.">
  <orders order_num="20005">
    <products prod_id="ANV01" prod_name=".5 ton anvil" />
    <products prod_id="ANV02" prod_name="1 ton anvil" />
    <products prod_id="FB" prod_name="Bird seed" />
    <products prod_id="TNT2" prod_name="TNT (5 sticks)" />
  </orders>
  <orders order_num="20009">
    <products prod_id="ANV03" prod_name="2 ton anvil" />
    <products prod_id="FB" prod_name="Bird seed" />
    <products prod_id="OL1" prod_name="Oil can" />
    <products prod_id="SLING" prod_name="Sling" />
  </orders>
</customers>
<customers cust_name="E Fudd">
  <orders order_num="20008">
    <products prod_id="FC" prod_name="Carrots" />
  </orders>
</customers>
<customers cust_name="Wascals">
  <orders order_num="20006">
    <products prod_id="JP2000" prod_name="JetPack 2000" />
  </orders>
</customers>
<customers cust_name="Yosemite Place">
  <orders order_num="20007">
    <products prod_id="TNT2" prod_name="TNT (5 sticks) " />
  </orders>
</customers>
```

Analysis ▼

Here, four tables are joined to return customers, orders placed by each customer, and the products in each order. The columns defined in the ORDER BY clause define the shape of the generated XML, resulting in a top-level <customers> tag containing one or more <orders> tags, which in turn contain one or more <products> tags.

Although AUTO may generate the desired XML, a bit more control is possible using the RAW format, as shown here:

Input ▼

```
SELECT vend_id AS id, RTrim(vend_name) AS name
FROM vendors
ORDER BY vend_name
FOR XML RAW('vendor'), ROOT('vendors'), ELEMENTS;
```

Output ▼

```
<vendors>
  <vendor>
    <id>1003</id>
    <name>ACME</name>
  </vendor>
  <vendor>
    <id>1001</id>
    <name>Anvils R Us</name>
  </vendor>
  <vendor>
    <id>1004</id>
    <name>Furball Inc.</name>
  </vendor>
  <vendor>
    <id>1005</id>
    <name>Jet Set</name>
  </vendor>
  <vendor>
    <id>1006</id>
    <name>Jouets Et Ours</name>
  </vendor>
  <vendor>
    <id>1002</id>
    <name>LT Supplies</name>
  </vendor>
</vendors>
```

Analysis ▼

This example demonstrates several useful techniques. The ELEMENTS keyword causes the columns to be embedded as child elements instead of tag attributes. RAW allows the row tag name to be specified, and ROOT is used to specify the top-level (root) name. In addition, column aliases are used to explicitly control the generated element names.

For even greater control, EXPLICIT mode can be used. EXPLICIT places the burden of forming the XML shape entirely on you, but in doing so it allows you to mix the use of elements and attributes, provide additional levels of nesting, and more. Here is an example:

Input ▼

```
SELECT 1 AS tag,
       NULL AS parent,
       vend_id AS [vendor!1!id],
       RTrim(vend_name) AS [vendor!1!name!ELEMENT]
FROM vendors
ORDER BY vend_name
FOR XML EXPLICIT, ROOT('vendors');
```

Output ▼

```
<vendors>
  <vendor id="1003">
    <name>ACME</name>
  </vendor>
  <vendor id="1001">
    <name>Anvils R Us</name>
  </vendor>
  <vendor id="1004">
    <name>Furball Inc.</name>
  </vendor>
  <vendor id="1005">
    <name>Jet Set</name>
  </vendor>
  <vendor id="1006">
    <name>Jouets Et Ours</name>
  </vendor>
  <vendor id="1002">
    <name>LT Supplies</name>
  </vendor>
</vendors>
```

Analysis ▼

When `EXPLICIT` is used, the `SELECT` statement must define a `tag` and a `parent`, and then the columns to be processed. Each column must be in the format `tagname!tagid!attributename`. In addition, optional attributes may be defined per column, as is the case with `vend_name`, which is renamed to `name` and defined as an `ELEMENT`.

> TIP: **XPath Is Another Option**
>
> XPath is a language used for accessing XML data. For the ideal combination of power and simplicity when generating XML, you may want to use `FOR XML PATH` mode, which allows you to define XPath expressions to structure the output. Unfortunately, coverage of XPath is beyond the scope of this book.

Storing XML Data

XML data is text containing nested tags in a strictly governed format. But XML is still just a string of text. As such, if you needed to save XML data into a table, you could use any column defined with a text datatype (preferably a variable-length datatype).

But doing so is not ideal. For starters, if the column allowed text to be stored, then even non-XML text could end up in the table, and that could seriously impede subsequent XML processing. In addition, manipulating and retrieving XML data stored as a string is far from ideal, because SQL Server cannot differentiate between the XML and the data stored in it.

For these and additional reasons, SQL Server 2005 introduced a new XML datatype. Here are some of the benefits of using this datatype:

- ▶ XML columns only accept well-formed XML; there is no way anything other than XML could get stored in them.

- ▶ Data in XML columns can be validated against an XML schema (a document that describes the format of a specific XML specification).

- ▶ Data in XML columns can be searched using XQuery searches.

> NOTE: **XQuery**
>
> XQuery is a query language used with XML. You can think of it like this: SQL is to relational databases what XQuery is to XML data. XQuery is not covered in this book.

Here is an example of a table with an XML datatype column:

Input ▼

```
CREATE TABLE MyXMLTable
(
    id   INT NOT NULL IDENTITY(1,1) PRIMARY KEY,
    data XML  NOT NULL
);
```

Analysis ▼

As explained in Lesson 20, "Creating and Manipulating Tables," CREATE TABLE is used to create new database tables. This CREATE TABLE statement creates a simple table with two columns, the second of which is of type XML.

Once the table is created, rows may be added to the table using INSERT. But care must be taken to ensure that the XML to be added is syntactically accurate.

Input ▼

```
INSERT INTO MyXMLTable(data)
VALUES(
'<state abbrev="CA">
  <city name="Los Angeles" />
  <city name="San Francisco" />
</state>');

INSERT INTO MyXMLTable(data)
VALUES(
'<state abbrev="IL">
  <city name="Chicago" />
</state>');
```

```
INSERT INTO MyXMLTable(data)
VALUES(
'<state abbrev="NY">
  <city name="New York" />
</state>');
```

Analysis ▼

Here, three rows are added to the table, each value as a string of text. Because the text is syntactically valid XML, the insertions are successful.

In practice, it is generally a good idea to convert a string containing XML to an actual XML datatype. Here is an example of this:

Input ▼

```
INSERT INTO MyXMLTable(data)
VALUES(
Cast('<state abbrev="CA">
  <city name="Los Angeles" />
  <city name="San Francisco" />
</state>' AS XML));

INSERT INTO MyXMLTable(data)
VALUES(
Cast('<state abbrev="IL">
  <city name="Chicago" />
</state>' AS XML));

INSERT INTO MyXMLTable(data)
VALUES(
Cast ('<state abbrev="NY">
  <city name="New York" />
</state>' AS XML));
```

Analysis ▼

This example inserts the same data, but firsts converts each string to XML using the Cast() function.

> **NOTE: Using XML Schemas**
> As already explained, an XML schema is a document that defines what a specific XML format should look like. XML schemas may be defined in SQL Server using CREATE XML SCHEMA. Once defined, schemas may be associated with XML datatype table columns. This way, whenever XML data is stored, SQL Server will not just ensure that it is well-formed, but will also validate it against the schema, ensuring that only valid XML is stored.

Searching for XML Data

Searching for XML data requires the use of XQuery. XML fields can be accessed using the following XML datatype methods (or functions):

- ▶ exist is used to check whether an XQuery expression exists.

- ▶ modify is used to modify XML contents.

- ▶ nodes is used to break apart XML records into multiple SQL rows.

- ▶ query is used to extract specific elements from XML records.

- ▶ value returns the SQL type from an XML record.

XQuery is not covered in this book. However, to give you an idea of what XQuery-based operations look like, here are a couple examples:

Input ▼

```
SELECT data.query('/state/city')
FROM MyXMLTable;
```

Analysis ▼

This example extracts the city names from the previously stored XML data. /state/city means "find a <state> tag and then find a child tag within it named <city>." Obviously, this type of data extraction would be much more complex if simple string processing had to be used.

Input ▼

```
SELECT *
FROM MyXMLTable
WHERE data.exist('/state/city[@name="Chicago"]') = 1;
```

Analysis ▼

This example locates rows containing a `<state>` tag with a child `<city>` tag named `Chicago`. Only one of the inserted rows matches this expression, so only it is returned.

As you can see, once data is stored as XML data (in an XML datatype column), XPath and XQuery can be used to perform very sophisticated data manipulation.

> TIP: **To Learn More**
>
> To learn more about XPath, visit http://www.w3.org/TR/xpath. To learn more about XQuery, visit http://www.w3.org/XML/Query/.

Summary

In this lesson, you learned how to generate XML output based on selected data. You were also introduced to the XML datatype and saw examples of how to store and access XML data.

LESSON 28

Globalization and Localization

In this lesson, you'll learn the basics of how SQL Server handles different character sets and languages, and how to work with different character sets in your T-SQL code.

Understanding Character Sets and Collation Sequences

Database tables are used to store and retrieve data. Different languages and character sets need to be stored and retrieved differently. As such, SQL Server needs to accommodate different character sets (different alphabets and characters) as well as different ways to sort and retrieve data.

When discussing multiple languages and characters sets, you will run into the following important terms:

- ▶ **Character sets:** Collections of letters and symbols

- ▶ **Encodings:** The internal representations of the members of a character set

- ▶ **Collations:** The instructions that dictate how characters are to be compared

> **NOTE: Why Collations Are Important**
> Sorting text in English is easy, right? Well, maybe not. Consider the words APE, apex, and Apple. Are they in the correct sorted order? That would depend on whether you wanted a case-sensitive or a non-case-sensitive sorting. The words would be sorted one way using a case-sensitive collation, and another way using a non-case-sensitive collation. And this affects more than just sorting (as in data sorted using ORDER BY); it also affects searches (whether or not a WHERE clause looking for apple finds APPLE, for example). The situation gets even more complex when characters such as the French à and German ö are used, and even more complex when non-Latin-based character sets are used (Japanese, Hebrew, Russian, and so on).

Working with Collation Sequences

SQL Server comes with hundreds of built-in collations sequences. To see the full list supported by your server, use the special fn_helpcollations() function, as shown here:

Input ▼

```
SELECT * FROM fn_helpcollations();
```

Analysis ▼

fn_helpcollations() returns a list of all available collations, with the name and description of each. You can use a WHERE clause to filter the list to find the exact collation you are looking for.

You will notice that several character sets have more than one collation. Latin1 General, for example, has many variants, and many appear twice, once case sensitive (designated by _CS) and once case insensitive (designated by _CI).

At SQL Server installation time, a default collation sequence is defined. You can determine the default collation sequence by using the ServerProperty() function, as shown here:

Input ▼

```
SELECT ServerProperty('Collation') AS Collation;
```

Output ▼

```
Collation
- - - - - - - - - - - - - - - - - - - - - - - - - - -
SQL_Latin1_General_CP1_CI_AS
```

Analysis ▼

This statement displays the current default server collation. (Your own server may display a collation other than the one shown in this output.)

As you will recall from Lesson 1, "Understanding SQL," when a database is created, a default collation sequence is defined for that database. Unless explicitly specified, this will be the same as the server default.

To determine the collation sequence defined for a specific database, you can use the server function DatabasePropertyEX():

Input ▼

```
SELECT DatabasePropertyEX('Crash Course', 'Collation')
     AS Collation;
```

Analysis ▼

This statement displays the default collation for the specified database.

To obtain more information about the named collation, you can use the previously mentioned fn_helpcollations() function, like this:

Input ▼

```
-- Get collation name
DECLARE @Collation VARCHAR(100);
SELECT @Collation = CONVERT(VARCHAR(100),
                              ServerProperty('Collation'))

-- Get description
SELECT description
FROM fn_helpcollations()
WHERE name = @Collation;
```

Analysis ▼

This example first obtains the server collation, as shown previously, and then uses `fn_helpcollations()` to obtain a collation `description`.

In practice, character sets can seldom be server-wide (or even database-wide) settings. Different table columns may require different character sets, and so these may be specified when a table is created.

To specify a character set and collation for a table, you use `CREATE TABLE` (discussed in Lesson 20, "Creating and Manipulating Tables") with additional clauses:

Input ▼

```
CREATE TABLE mytable
(
    column1   INT,
    column2   VARCHAR(10) COLLATE Hebrew_CI_AI
);
```

Analysis ▼

This statement creates a two-column table and specifies a specific collation sequence for one of the columns.

> TIP: **Changing Collations**
>
> You can change collations after table creation by using ALTER TABLE.

Managing Case Sensitivity

One very important use of collation sequences is to change how case is handled when searching and sorting. The default collation sequences usually make searches and sorting case insensitive. If a specific column always needs case-sensitive searches and sorting, that column can be defined to use a case-sensitive collation sequence:

Input ▼

```
CREATE TABLE mytable
(
    column1    INT,
    column2    VARCHAR(10) COLLATE SQL_Latin1_General_CP1_CS_AS
);
```

If you need to sort specific SELECT statements using a collation sequence other than the one used at table-creation time, you may do so in the SELECT statement itself:

Input ▼

```
SELECT * FROM customers
ORDER BY cust_name COLLATE SQL_Latin1_General_CP1_CS_AS;
```

Analysis ▼

This SELECT uses COLLATE to specify an alternate collation sequence (in this example, a case-sensitive one). This will obviously affect the order in which results are sorted.

> TIP: **Occasional Case Sensitivity**
>
> The SELECT statement just shown demonstrates a useful technique for performing case-sensitive searches on a table that is usually not case sensitive. And of course, the reverse works just as well.

Alternate collation sequences can also be used in WHERE clauses to change the case sensitivity of searches. Here is a simple wildcard search:

Input ▼

```
SELECT cust_id, cust_name
FROM customers
WHERE cust_name LIKE '%E%'
```

Output ▼

```
cust_id      cust_name
-----------  --------------
10001        Coyote Inc.
10002        Mouse House
10004        Yosemite Place
10005        E Fudd
10006        Pep E. LaPew
10007        Pep E. LaPew
```

Analysis ▼

This SELECT retrieves all rows with an E in cust_name, regardless of whether the E is upper- or lowercase.

Now for a case-sensitive search:

Input ▼

```
SELECT cust_id, cust_name
FROM customers
WHERE cust_name COLLATE SQL_Latin1_General_CP1_CS_AS LIKE '%E%'
```

Output ▼

```
cust_id      cust_name
-----------  --------------
10005        E Fudd
10006        Pep E. LaPew
10007        Pep E. LaPew
```

Analysis ▼

This SELECT uses COLLATE to specify a case-sensitive collation sequence, so only rows with an uppercase E in cust_name are retrieved.

Working with Unicode

Unicode is a mechanism by which differing character sets (particularly
non-Latin-based character sets) are referenced and stored. Working with
Unicode text in SQL Server requires the following:

▶ To successfully store these characters in SQL Server tables, the
columns must be of a type that can store Unicode text.

▶ Unicode versions of functions should be used, for example,
NChar() instead of Char().

▶ Any time Unicode text is passed to a T-SQL statement, it must
be designated as such.

SQL Server defines three special datatypes specifically for storing
Unicode text: NCHAR (Unicode equivalent of CHAR), NVARCHAR (Unicode
equivalent of VARCHAR), and NTEXT (Unicode equivalent of TEXT).

Once a column is defined as supporting Unicode text, you still need to tell
SQL Server that the text being used in Unicode. And you must do this
every time you pass strings to T-SQL.

Consider these examples:

Input ▼

```
INSERT INTO mytable(column1, column2)
VALUES(1000, 'שלום');
SELECT * FROM mytable;
```

Output ▼

```
column1      column2
----------   ----------
1000         ????
```

Analysis ▼

This INSERT statement inserts a row with non-Latin text (Hebrew, in this example) into the previously created mytable. But when retrieved, the text is displayed as ????. In other words, SQL Server did not recognize it as Unicode and it was therefore not stored properly.

Here's the right way to do it:

Input ▼

```
INSERT INTO mytable(column1, column2)
VALUES(1000, N'שלום');
SELECT * FROM mytable;
```

Output ▼

```
column1      column2
----------   ----------
1000         שלום
```

Analysis ▼

This INSERT statement inserts the same text, but prefixes the string with N to tell SQL Server to treat the text that follows as Unicode. This way, the data is stored properly, and the subsequent SELECT retrieves the correct data.

> **CAUTION: Always Remember the N Prefix**
>
> The N prefix *must* be specified whenever Unicode strings are used, be it text passed to INSERT or UPDATE, or even strings used in a WHERE clause.

Summary

In this lesson, you learned the basics of character sets and collations. You also learned how to define the character sets and collations for specific tables and columns, how to use alternate collations when needed, and how to handle Unicode text.

LESSON 29

Managing Security

Database servers usually contain critical data, and ensuring the safety and integrity of that data requires that access control be used. In this lesson, you'll learn about SQL Server access control and user management.

Understanding Access Control

The basis of security for your SQL Server is this: *Users should have appropriate access to the data they need, no more and no less.* In other words, users should not have too much access to too much data.

Consider the following:

- ▶ Most users need to read and write data from tables, but few users will ever need to be able to create and drop tables.

- ▶ Some users might need to read tables but might not need to update them.

- ▶ You might want to allow users to add data, but not delete data.

- ▶ Some users (managers or administrators) might need rights to manipulate user accounts, but most should not.

- ▶ You might want users to access data via stored procedures, but never directly.

- ▶ You might want to restrict access to some functionality based on where the user is logging in.

These are just examples, but they help demonstrate an important point. You need to provide users with the access they need and just the access they need. This is known as *access control*, and managing access control requires creating and managing user accounts.

> TIP: **Use the Administration Tools**
>
> The SQL Server tools (described in Lesson 2, "Introducing SQL Server") provide a graphical user interface that can be used to manage users and account rights. Internally, these tools actually use the statements described in this lesson, enabling you to manage access control interactively and simply.

Back in Lesson 3, "Working with SQL Server," you learned that you need to log in to SQL Server in order to perform any operations. When first installed, SQL Server creates a user account named sa (for System Administrator), which has complete and total control over the entire SQL Server. You might have been using the sa login throughout the lessons in this book, and that is fine when experimenting with SQL Server on non-live servers. But in the real world you'd never use sa on a day-to-day basis. Instead, you'd create a series of accounts, some for administration, some for users, some for developers, and so on.

> NOTE: **Preventing Innocent Mistakes**
>
> It is important to note that access control is not just intended to keep out users with malicious intent. More often than not, data nightmares are the result of an inadvertent mistake, a mistyped T-SQL statement, being in the wrong database, or some other user error. Access control helps avoid these situations by ensuring that users are unable to execute statements they should not be executing.

> CAUTION: **Don't Use** sa
>
> The sa login should be considered sacred. Use it only when absolutely needed (perhaps if you cannot get in to other administrative accounts). sa should never be used in day-to-day SQL Server operations.

Managing Users

> NOTE: **Windows or SQL Server?**
>
> SQL Server supports two forms of logins and accounts. It can use its own list of users and accounts, or it can leverage the accounts managed by the underlying Windows operating system (or Windows domain, if the server is part of one).
>
> User management, as described in this section, only applies to SQL Server logins, and not to Windows logins. If you are using Windows logins, then account creation, deletion, password changes, and more, should be managed using Windows administrative tools.
>
> However, access control and permissions are always managed within SQL Server.

SQL Server user accounts and information are stored in the internal SYS database. You usually do not need to access the SYS database and tables directly. Instead, SQL Server comes with a series of stored procedures that manipulate the SYS tables for you.

For example, to obtain a list of logins, you could retrieve data from SYS tables, or you could use the sp_helplogins stored procedure:

Input ▼

```
EXEC sp_helplogins;
```

Analysis ▼

sp_helplogins returns two result sets. The first lists each login and information about each. The second lists users associated with logins.

> TIP: **Listing Specific Logins**
>
> sp_helplogins lists all logins. To display a specific login, pass that login name as a parameter to the stored procedure.

Creating User Accounts

To create a new user login, use the CREATE LOGIN statement, as shown here:

Input ▼

```
CREATE LOGIN BenF WITH PASSWORD = 'P@$$w0rd';
```

Analysis ▼

CREATE LOGIN creates a new user login. A password need not be specified at user account creation time, but this example does specify a password.

If you were to list the user accounts again, you'd see the new account listed in the output.

> NOTE: **Pre–SQL Server 2005**
>
> The CREATE LOGIN statement was introduced in SQL Server 2005. If you are using an earlier version of SQL Server, you should use the sp_addlogin stored procedure instead, like this:
>
> ```
> EXEC sp_addlogin 'BenF', ' P@$$w0rd ';
> ```

Deleting User Accounts

To delete a login (along with any associated rights and privileges), use the DROP LOGIN statement, as shown here:

Input ▼

```
DROP LOGIN BenF;
```

Enabling and Disabling Accounts

To disable an account (without deleting it), use ALTER LOGIN, as shown here:

Input ▼

```
ALTER LOGIN BenF DISABLE;
```

To enable a disabled account, do the following:

Input ▼

```
ALTER LOGIN BenF ENABLE;
```

Renaming Logins

To rename a login, use ALTER TABLE, as shown here:

Input ▼

```
ALTER LOGIN BenF WITH NAME = BenForta;
```

Changing Passwords

To change user passwords, use ALTER LOGIN, as shown here:

Input ▼

```
ALTER LOGIN BenF WITH PASSWORD = 'n3w p@$$w0rd';
```

Managing Access Rights

Once a login has been created, you need to specify what databases, tables, and functionality it has access to. Doing so involves setting and managing access rights.

NOTE: Refer to SQL Server Documentation

The full list of rights that can be granted is beyond the scope of this book. This is true of all versions of SQL Server. And SQL Server 2005 has significantly enhanced the list of possible grants and their level of granularity. With the basics explained here, refer to SQL Server documentation for more details and specifics.

Setting Access Rights

To set rights, you use the GRANT statement. At a minimum, GRANT requires that you specify the following:

- ▶ The privilege being granted
- ▶ The database or table being granted access to
- ▶ The user name

The following example demonstrates the use of GRANT:

Input ▼

```
GRANT CREATE TABLE TO BenF;
```

Analysis ▼

This GRANT allows the use of CREATE TABLE. By being granted CREATE TABLE access only, user BenF can create new tables, but not alter or drop existing tables.

> NOTE: **Allowing the Granted to Grant**
> When using GRANT, you may specify the WITH GRANT OPTION clause so as to allow the user to grant this same access to others.

Removing Access Rights

The opposite of GRANT is REVOKE, which is used to revoke specific rights and permissions. Here is an example:

Input ▼

```
REVOKE CREATE TABLE FROM BenF;
```

Analysis ▼

This REVOKE statement takes away the CREATE TABLE access just granted to user BenF.

GRANT and REVOKE can be used to control access at several levels:

- ▶ Entire server
- ▶ Entire database
- ▶ Specific tables
- ▶ Specific columns
- ▶ Specific stored procedures

Summary

In this lesson, you learned about access control and how to secure your SQL Server by managing user logins and assigning specific rights to users.

LESSON 30

Improving Performance

In this lesson, you'll review some important points pertaining to the performance of SQL Server.

Improving Performance

Database administrators spend a significant portion of their lives tweaking and experimenting to improve DBMS performance. Poorly performing databases (and database queries, for that matter) tend to be the most frequent culprits when diagnosing application sluggishness and performance problems.

What follows is not, by any stretch of the imagination, the last word on SQL Server performance. This is intended to review key points made in the previous 29 lessons, as well as to provide a springboard from which to launch performance optimization discussion and analysis.

So, here goes:

- ▶ First and foremost, SQL Server (like all DBMSs) has specific hardware recommendations. Using any old computer as a database server is fine when you are learning and playing with SQL Server. But production servers should adhere to all recommendations.

- ▶ As a rule, critical production DBMSs should run on their own dedicated servers.

- ▶ SQL Server is preconfigured with a series of default settings that are usually a good place to start. But after a while you might need to tweak memory allocation, buffer sizes, and more.

> TIP: **Use SQL Server 2005 Tuning Advisor**
>
> SQL Server 2005 comes with a wonderful utility named Database Engine Tuning Advisor, which can be run from with the Microsoft SQL Server Management Studio (under the Tools menu). This utility can analyze your database and tables and make recommendations about indexes, partitions, and more. This tool is specifically designed for users who don't want to learn all of the complexities of SQL Server internals. It should definitely be taken advantage of.

- ▶ SQL Server is a multiuser, multithreaded DBMS; in other words, it often performs multiple tasks at the same time. And if one of those tasks is executing slowly, all requests will suffer. You can use Windows System Monitor to monitor SQL Server disk and memory usage, be alerted of critical events, and more.

- ▶ There is almost always more than one way to write a SELECT statement. Experiment with joins, unions, subqueries, and more to find what is optimum for you and your data.

- ▶ When SQL Server processes T-SQL statements, it attempts to optimize them, breaking requests into smaller requests as appropriate, using indexes, and so on. Understanding what SQL Server has done, and being able to determine the amount of time spent processing specific parts of a batch or stored procedure, is vital in optimizing performance. SQL Server can report the execution plan used by submitted SQL statements. This option is available in Microsoft SQL Server Management Studio (if you're using SQL Server 2005) and Enterprise Manager (if you're using an earlier version of SQL Server).

- ▶ As a general rule, stored procedures execute quicker than individual T-SQL statements.

- ▶ Use the right datatypes...always.

- ▶ Never retrieve more data than you need. In other words, don't use SELECT * (unless you truly do need each and every column).

- ▶ Database tables must be indexed to improve the performance of data retrieval. Determining what to index is not a trivial task, and involves analyzing used SELECT statements to find recurring WHERE and ORDER BY clauses. If a simple WHERE clause is taking too long to return results, you can bet that the column (or columns) being used is a good candidate for indexing.

- ▶ Have a series of complex OR conditions in your SELECT? You may see a significant performance improvement by using multiple SELECT statements and UNION to connect then.

- ▶ Indexes improve the performance of data retrieval, but hurt the performance of data insertion, deletion, and updating. If you have tables that collect data and are not often searched, don't index them until needed. (Indexes can be added and dropped as needed).

- ▶ LIKE is slow. As a general rule, you are better off using full-text searching with FREETEXT or CONTAINS.

- ▶ Databases are living entities. A well-optimized set of tables might not be so after a while. As table usage and contents change, so might the ideal optimization and configuration.

- ▶ And the most important rule is simply this: Every rule is meant to be broken at some point.

TIP: **Browse the Docs**

The SQL Server documentation installed with SQL Server is chock full of useful tips and tricks, and is completely searchable (and searches can also automatically include online resources). Be sure to check out this invaluable resource.

Summary

In this lesson, you reviewed some important tips and notes pertaining to SQL Server performance. Of course, this is just the tip of the iceberg, but now that you have completed this book, you are free to experiment and learn as you best see fit.

APPENDIX A

Getting Started with SQL Server and T-SQL

If you are new to SQL Server and T-SQL, here is what you need to know to get started.

What You'll Need

To start using T-SQL and to follow along with the lessons in this book, you need access to a SQL Server and copies of client applications (software used to access the server).

You do not need your own installed copy of SQL Server, but you do need access to a server. You basically have two options:

- ▶ Obtain access to an existing SQL Server installation, perhaps one by your hosting company or place of business or school. To use this server you will be granted a server account (a login name and password).

- ▶ Download and install a free copy of SQL Server Express for installation on your own computer (SQL Server runs on Windows machines only).

> TIP: **If You Can, Install a Local Server**
>
> For complete control, including access to commands and features that you will probably not be granted if using someone else's SQL Server, install your own local server. Even if you don't end up using your local server as your final production DBMS, you'll still benefit from having complete and unfettered access to all the server has to offer.

Regardless of whether you use a local server, you need client software (the program you use to actually run T-SQL commands). Your best option is to use the client programs that come with SQL Server:

► If you are using SQL Server 2005, the tool you want to use is SQL Server Management Studio.

► If you are using an earlier version of SQL Server, the tool you want to use is SQL Enterprise Manager (which includes a tool called Query Analyzer, where you actually execute T-SQL queries).

Obtaining the Software

To learn more about SQL Server, go to http://www.microsoft.com/sql/. This page contains links to trial software and other downloads. The trial software version of SQL Server 2005 is the full product, but it will only run for 180 days. SQL Server 2005 Express lacks some advanced functionality, but it's completely free to download and use.

NOTE: **SQL Server Express**

Although SQL Server Express does lack some of the more advanced features found in the commercial versions of SQL Server, this will not impact your studying with this book. All of the lessons in this book will work with the free SQL Server Express.

Installing the Software

Installing SQL Server is straightforward; the installation wizard will walk you through the process, which includes the following options:

► Setting an installation location. (The default is usually fine.)

► Choosing a password for the sa user.

- ▶ Installing the documentation. (You are strongly encouraged to do so.)

- ▶ Selecting from lots of other options. (You can generally use the default values.)

Preparing for Your Lessons

After you have installed SQL Server, Lesson 3, "Working with SQL Server," shows you how to log in and log out of the server, and how to execute commands.

The lessons in this book all use real T-SQL statements and real data. Appendix B, "The Example Tables," describes the example tables used in this book, and explains how to obtain and use the table-creation and population scripts.

APPENDIX B

The Example Tables

Writing SQL statements requires a good understanding of the underlying database design. Without knowing what information is stored in what table, how tables are related to each other, and the actual breakup of data within a row, it is impossible to write effective SQL.

You are strongly advised to actually try every example in every lesson in this book. All the lessons use a common set of data files. To assist you in better understanding the examples and to enable you to follow along with the lessons, this appendix describes the tables used, their relationships, and how to obtain them.

Understanding the Example Tables

The tables used throughout this book are part of an order-entry system used by an imaginary distributor of paraphernalia that might be needed by your favorite cartoon characters (yes, cartoon characters; no one said that learning T-SQL needed to be boring). The tables are used to perform several tasks:

► Manage vendors

► Manage product catalogs

► Manage customer lists

► Enter customer orders

Making this all work requires six tables that are closely interconnected as part of a relational database design. A description of each of the tables appears in the following sections.

> **NOTE: Simplified Examples**
> The tables used here are by no means complete. A real-world order-entry system would have to keep track of lots of other data that has not been included here (for example, payment and accounting information, shipment tracking, and more). However, these tables do demonstrate the kinds of data organization and relationships you will encounter in most real installations. You can apply these techniques and technologies to your own databases.

Table Descriptions

What follows is a description of each of the six tables, along with the name of the columns within each table and their descriptions.

> **NOTE: Why Out of Order?**
> If you are wondering why the six tables are listed in the order they are, it is due to their dependencies. Because the products tables is dependent on the vendors table, vendors is listed first, and so on.

The vendors Table

The vendors table stores the vendors whose products are sold. Every vendor has a record in this table, and that vendor ID (the vend_id) column is used to match products with vendors.

TABLE B.1 vendors Table Columns

Column	Description
vend_id	Unique numeric vendor ID
vend_name	Vendor name
vend_address	Vendor address
vend_city	Vendor city
vend_state	Vendor state
vend_zip	Vendor ZIP Code
vend_country	Vendor country

► All tables should have primary keys defined. This table should use vend_id as its primary key. vend_id is an identity field.

The products Table

The products table contains the product catalog, one product per row. Each product has a unique ID (the prod_id column) and is related to its vendor by vend_id (the vendor's unique ID).

TABLE B.2 products Table Columns

Column	Description
prod_id	Unique product ID
vend_id	Product vendor ID (relates to vend_id in vendors table)
prod_name	Product name
prod_price	Product price
prod_desc	Product description

► All tables should have primary keys defined. This table should use prod_id as its primary key.

► To enforce referential integrity, a foreign key should be defined on vend_id, relating it to vend_id in vendors.

The customers Table

The customers table stores all customer information. Each customer has a unique ID (the cust_id column).

TABLE B.3 customers Table Columns

Column	Description
cust_id	Unique numeric customer ID
cust_name	Customer name
cust_address	Customer address
cust_city	Customer city
cust_state	Customer state

continues

TABLE B.3 Continued

Column	Description
cust_zip	Customer ZIP Code
cust_country	Customer country
cust_contact	Customer contact name
cust_email	Customer contact email address

- ▶ All tables should have primary keys defined. This table should use cust_id as its primary key. cust_id is an identity field.

The orders Table

The orders table stores customer orders (but not order details). Each order is uniquely numbered (the order_num column). Orders are associated with the appropriate customers by the cust_id column (which relates to the customer's unique ID in the customers table).

TABLE B.4 orders Table Columns

Column	Description
order_num	Unique order number
order_date	Order date
cust_id	Order customer ID (relates to cust_id in customers table)

- ▶ All tables should have primary keys defined. This table should use order_num as its primary key. order_num is an identity field.
- ▶ To enforce referential integrity, a foreign key should be defined on cust_id, relating it to cust_id in customers.

The orderitems Table

The orderitems table stores the actual items in each order, one row per item per order. For every row in orders there are one or more rows in orderitems. Each order item is uniquely identified by the order number plus the order item (first item in order, second item in order, and so on). Order items are associated with their appropriate order by the order_num column (which relates to the order's unique ID in orders). In addition, each order item contains the product ID of the item orders (which relates the item back to the products table).

TABLE B.5 orderitems Table Columns

Column	Description
order_num	Order number (relates to order_num in orders table)
order_item	Order item number (sequential within an order)
prod_id	Product ID (relates to prod_id in products table)
quantity	Item quantity
item_price	Item price

► All tables should have primary keys defined. This table should use order_num and order_item as its primary keys.

► To enforce referential integrity, foreign keys should be defined on order_num, relating it to order_num in orders, and prod_id, relating it to prod_id in products.

The productnotes Table

The productnotes table stores notes associated with specific products. Not all products may have associated notes, and some products may have many associated notes.

TABLE B.6 productnotes Table Columns

Column	Description
note_id	Unique note ID
prod_id	Product ID (corresponds to prod_id in products table)
note_date	Date note was added
note_text	Note text

► All tables should have primary keys defined. This table should use note_id as its primary key.

► To enforce referential integrity, a foreign key should be defined on prod_id, relating it to prod_id in products.

Creating the Example Tables

In order to follow along with the examples, you need a set of populated tables. Everything you need to get up and running can be found on this book's web page at

http://www.forta.com/books/0672328674/

The web page contains two SQL script files that you may download:

- create.sql contains the T-SQL statements to create the six database tables (including defining all primary keys and foreign key constraints).

- populate.sql contains the SQL INSERT statements used to populate these tables.

> **NOTE: For SQL Server Only**
>
> The SQL statements in the downloadable .sql files are very DBMS specific and are designed to be used only with Microsoft SQL Server.
>
> The scripts have been tested extensively with SQL Server 2000 and SQL Server 2005 and have not been tested with earlier versions of SQL Server.

After you have downloaded the scripts, you can use them to create and populate the tables needed to follow along with the lessons in this book. Here are the steps to follow:

1. Create a new database named crashcourse (or pick any name of your choice, but do not use any existing database name, just to be on the safe side). If you're using SQL Server 2005, the simplest way to do this is to use the Microsoft SQL Server Management Studio (described in Lesson 2, "Introducing SQL Server"). If you're using SQL Server 2000, use SQL Enterprise Manager.

2. Make sure the new database is selected (use the USE command, or select the database from the drop-down list). If you're using the Microsoft SQL Server Management Studio, you can do this

right inside of the same tool. If you're using SQL Server 2000, use SQL Query Analyzer.

3. Execute the `create.sql` script. You may simply copy and paste the entire contents of the file into the query window, or you can use the File menu options to open `create.sql` directly. (If you're using SQL Server 2005, you should be able to just double-click files with an `.sql` extension to open them in Microsoft SQL Server Management Studio).

4. Repeat the previous step using the `populate.sql` file to populate the new tables.

And with that you should be good to go!

> **NOTE: Create, Then Populate**
> You must run the table-creation scripts *before* the table-population scripts. Be sure to check for any error messages returned by these scripts. If the creation scripts fail, you will need to remedy whatever problem might exist before continuing with table population.

APPENDIX C

T-SQL Statement Syntax

To help you find the syntax you need when you need it, this appendix lists the syntax for the most frequently used T-SQL operations. Each statement starts with a brief description and then displays the appropriate syntax. For added convenience, you'll also find cross-references to the lessons where specific statements are taught.

When reading statement syntax, remember the following:

- ▶ The ¦ symbol is used to indicate one of several options, so NULL¦NOT NULL means specify either NULL or NOT NULL.

- ▶ Keywords or clauses contained within square parentheses [like this] are optional.

- ▶ Not all T-SQL statements are listed, nor is every clause and option listed.

BEGIN TRANSACTION

BEGIN TRANSACTION is used to start a new transaction block. See Lesson 26, "Managing Transaction Processing," for more information.

Input ▼

```
BEGIN TRANSACTION;
```

ALTER TABLE

ALTER TABLE is used to update the schema of an existing table. To create a new table, use CREATE TABLE. See Lesson 20, "Creating and Manipulating Tables," for more information.

Input ▼

```
ALTER TABLE tablename
(
    ADD        column          datatype    [NULL|NOT NULL]
                                           [CONSTRAINTS],
    ALTER      column columns   datatype    [NULL|NOT NULL]
                                           [CONSTRAINTS],
    DROP       column,
    ...
);
```

COMMIT TRANSACTION

COMMIT TRANSACTION is used to write a transaction to the database. See Lesson 26 for more information.

Input ▼

```
COMMIT TRANSACTION;
```

CREATE INDEX

CREATE INDEX is used to create an index on one or more columns. See Lesson 20 for more information.

Input ▼

```
CREATE INDEX indexname
ON tablename (column [ASC|DESC], ...);
```

CREATE LOGIN

CREATE LOGIN is used to add a new user account to the system. See Lesson 29, "Managing Security," for more information.

Input ▼

```
CREATE LOGIN loginname;
```

CREATE PROCEDURE

CREATE PROCEDURE is used to create .a stored procedure. See Lesson 23, "Working with Stored Procedures," for more information.

Input ▼

```
CREATE PROCEDURE procedurename
[parameters]
AS
BEGIN
...
END;
```

CREATE TABLE

CREATE TABLE is used to create new database tables. To update the schema of an existing table, use ALTER TABLE. See Lesson 20 for more information.

Input ▼

```
CREATE TABLE tablename
(
    column    datatype    [NULL¦NOT NULL]    [CONSTRAINTS],
    column    datatype    [NULL¦NOT NULL]    [CONSTRAINTS],
    ...
);
```

CREATE VIEW

CREATE VIEW is used to create a new view of one or more tables. See
Lesson 21, "Using Views," for more information.

Input ▼

```
CREATE VIEW viewname
AS
SELECT ...;
```

DELETE

DELETE deletes one or more rows from a table. See Lesson 19, "Updating
and Deleting Data," for more information.

Input ▼

```
DELETE FROM tablename
[WHERE ...];
```

DROP

DROP permanently removes database objects (tables, views, indexes, and
so forth). See Lessons 20, 21, and 23, as well as Lesson 24, "Using
Cursors," and Lesson 25, "Using Triggers," for more information.

Input ▼

```
DROP DATABASE|INDEX|LOGIN|PROCEDURE|TABLE|TRIGGER|VIEW
    itemname;
```

INSERT

INSERT adds a single row to a table. See Lesson 18, "Inserting Data," for
more information.

Input ▼

```
INSERT INTO tablename [(columns, ...)]
VALUES(values, ...);
```

INSERT SELECT

INSERT SELECT inserts the results of a SELECT into a table. See Lesson 18 for more information.

Input ▼

```
INSERT INTO tablename [(columns, ...)]
SELECT columns, ... FROM tablename, ...
[WHERE ...];
```

ROLLBACK TRANSACTION

ROLLBACK TRANSACTION is used to undo a transaction block. See Lesson 26 for more information.

Input ▼

```
ROLLBACK [savepointname];
```

SAVE TRANSACTION

SAVE TRANSACTION defines a savepoint for use with a ROLLBACK statement. See Lesson 26 for more information.

Input ▼

```
SAVE TRANSACTION sp1;
```

SELECT

SELECT is used to retrieve data from one or more tables (or views). See Lesson 4, "Retrieving Data," Lesson 5, "Sorting Retrieved Data," and Lesson 6, "Filtering Data," for more basic information. (Lessons 4–17 all cover aspects of SELECT.)

Input ▼

```
SELECT columnname, ...
FROM tablename, ...
[WHERE ...]
[UNION ...]
[GROUP BY ...]
[HAVING ...]
[ORDER BY ...];
```

UPDATE

UPDATE updates one or more rows in a table. See Lesson 19 for more information.

Input ▼

```
UPDATE tablename
SET columnname = value, ...
[WHERE ...];
```

APPENDIX D

T-SQL Datatypes

As explained in Lesson 1, "Understanding SQL," datatypes are basically rules that define what data may be stored in a column and how that data is actually stored.

Datatypes are used for several reasons:

- ▶ Datatypes enable you to restrict the type of data that can be stored in a column. For example, a numeric datatype column only accepts numeric values.

- ▶ Datatypes allow for more efficient storage, internally. Numbers and date/time values can be stored in a more condensed format than text strings.

- ▶ Datatypes allow for alternate sorting orders. If everything is treated as strings, 1 comes before 10, which comes before 2. (Strings are sorted in dictionary sequence, one character at a time starting from the left.) As numeric datatypes, the numbers would be sorted correctly.

When designing tables, pay careful attention to the datatypes being used. Using the wrong datatype can seriously impact your application. Changing the datatypes of existing populated columns is not a trivial task. (In addition, doing so can result in data loss.)

Although this appendix is by no means a complete tutorial on datatypes and how they are to be used, it explains the major T-SQL datatype types and what they are used for.

String Datatypes

The most commonly used datatypes are string datatypes. These datatypes store strings (for example, names, addresses, phone numbers, and ZIP Codes). As shown in Table D.1, there are basically two types of string datatypes you can use: fixed-length strings and variable-length strings.

Fixed-length strings are datatypes defined to accept a fixed number of characters, and that number is specified when the table is created. For example, you might allow 30 characters in a "first name" column or 11 characters in a "social security number" column (the exact number needed allowing for the two dashes). Fixed-length columns do not allow more than the specified number of characters. They also allocate storage space for as many characters as specified. So, if the string Ben is stored in a 30-character "first name" field, a full 30 bytes are stored. CHAR is an example of a fixed-length string type.

Variable-length strings store text of variable lengths. TEXT is an example of a variable-length string type.

If variable-length datatypes are so flexible, why would you ever want to use fixed-length datatypes? The answer is performance. SQL Server can sort and manipulate fixed-length columns far more quickly than it can sort variable-length columns. In addition, SQL Server does not allow you to index variable-length columns (or the variable portion of a column). This also dramatically affects performance.

TABLE D.1 String Datatypes

Datatype	Description
CHAR	Fixed-length string from 1 to 8,000 characters long. Its size must be specified at create time; otherwise, SQL Server assumes CHAR(1).
NCHAR	Fixed-length Unicode string from 1 to 4,000 chars long. Its size must be specified at create time; otherwise, SQL Server assumes NCHAR(1).
NTEXT	Variable-length Unicode text with a maximum size of 1,073,741,823 characters.
NVARCHAR	Variable-length Unicode text with a maximum size of 4,000 characters.

TABLE D.1   Continued

Datatype	Description
TEXT	Variable-length text with a maximum size of 2,147,483,647 characters.
VARCHAR	Variable-length text with a maximum size of 8,000 characters.

> **TIP: Using Quotes**
>
> Regardless of the form of string datatype being used, string values must always be surrounded by quotes (single quotes are often preferred).

> **CAUTION: When Numeric Values Are Not Numeric Values**
>
> You might think that phone numbers and U.S. ZIP Codes should be stored in numeric fields (after all, they only store numeric data), but doing so would not be advisable. If you store the ZIP Code 01234 in a numeric field, the number 1234 would be saved. You'd actually lose a digit.
>
> The basic rule to follow is, if the number is used in calculations (sums, averages, and so on), it belongs in a numeric datatype column. If it is used as a literal string (that happens to contain only digits), it belongs in a string datatype column.

Numeric Datatypes

Numeric datatypes store numbers. SQL Server supports several numeric datatypes, each with a different range of numbers that can be stored in it. Obviously, the larger the supported range, the more storage space needed. In addition, some numeric datatypes support the use of decimal points (and fractional numbers), whereas others support only whole numbers. Table D.2 lists the frequently used SQL Server numeric datatypes.

TABLE D.2 Numeric Datatypes

Datatype	Description
BIT	A bit field, with a possible value of 0 or 1.
BIGINT	Integer value. Supports numbers from -9,223,372,036,854,775,808 to -9,223,372,036,854,775,807.
DECIMAL (or DEC or NUMERIC)	Floating-point value with varying levels of precision.
FLOAT	Variable-length byte floating-point value.
INT (or INTEGER)	Integer value. Supports numbers from -2,147,483,648 to 2,147,483,647.
MONEY	Currency with four decimal places. Supports numbers from -922,337,203,685,477.5808 to 922,337,203,685,477.5807.
REAL	Four-byte floating-point value.
SMALLINT	Integer value. Supports numbers from -32,768 to 32,767.
SMALLMONEY	Currency with four decimal places. Supports numbers from -214,748.3648 to 214,748.3647.
TINYINT	Integer value. Supports numbers from 0 to 255.

> TIP: **Not Using Quotes**
>
> Unlike strings, numeric values should never be enclosed within quotes.

Date and Time Datatypes

SQL Server uses special datatypes for the storage of date and time values, as listed in Table D.3.

TABLE D.3 Date and Time Datatypes

Datatype	Description
DATETIME	Stores dates from January 1, 1753 through December 31, 9999.
SMALLDATETIME	Stores dates from January 1, 1900 through June 6, 2079.

Binary Datatypes

Binary datatypes are used to store all sorts of data (even binary information), such as graphic images, multimedia, and word processing documents (see Table D.4).

TABLE D.4 Binary Datatypes

Datatype	Description
BINARY	Fixed-length binary data of up to 8,000 characters.
VARBINARY	Variable-length binary data of up to 8,000 characters.
VARBINARY(max)	Variable-length binary data exceeding 8,000 characters.

Other Datatypes

In addition to the datatypes listed thus far, SQL Server supports several special-purpose datatypes (see Table D.5).

TABLE D.5 Other Datatypes

Datatype	Description
CURSOR	Contains a reference to a cursor
TABLE	A temporary table
UNIQUEIDENTIFIER	A unique identifier in 16-byte GUID format
XML	Well-formed XML data

> NOTE: **Datatypes in Use**
>
> If you would like to see a real-world example of how different databases are used, see the sample table-creation scripts described in Appendix B, "The Example Tables."

APPENDIX E

T-SQL Reserved Words

The T-SQL implementation of SQL is made up of *keywords*; special words that are used in performing SQL operations. Special care must be taken not to use these keywords when you are naming databases, tables, columns, and any other database objects. Thus, these keywords are considered reserved. This appendix lists all of the T-SQL reserved words (as of SQL Server 2005), including ODBC reserved keywords as well as words that Microsoft has reserved for future use.

ABSOLUTE	ASSERTION	BULK
ACTION	AT	BY
ADA	AUTHORIZATION	CALL
ADD	AVG	CASCADE
ADMIN	BACKUP	CASCADED
AFTER	BEFORE	CASE
AGGREGATE	BEGIN	CAST
ALIAS	BETWEEN	CATALOG
ALL	BINARY	CHAR
ALLOCATE	BIT	CHAR_LENGTH
ALTER	BIT_LENGTH	CHARACTER
AND	BLOB	CHARACTER_LENGTH
ANY	BOOLEAN	CHECK
ARE	BOTH	CHECKPOINT
ARRAY	BREADTH	CLASS
AS	BREAK	CLOB
ASC	BROWSE	CLOSE

CLUSTERED	CURSOR	DISTRIBUTED
COALESCE	CYCLE	DOMAIN
COLLATE	DATA	DOUBLE
COLLATION	DATABASE	DROP
COLUMN	DATE	DUMMY
COMMIT	DAY	DUMP
COMPLETION	DBCC	DYNAMIC
COMPUTE	DEALLOCATE	EACH
CONNECT	DEC	ELSE
CONNECTION	DECIMAL	END
CONSTRAINT	DECLARE	END-EXEC
CONSTRAINTS	DEFAULT	EQUALS
CONSTRUCTOR	DEFERRABLE	ERRLVL
CONTAINS	DEFERRED	ESCAPE
CONTAINSTABLE	DELETE	EVERY
CONTINUE	DENY	EXCEPT
CONVERT	DEPTH	EXCEPTION
CORRESPONDING	DEREF	EXEC
COUNT	DESC	EXECUTE
CREATE	DESCRIBE	EXISTS
CROSS	DESCRIPTOR	EXIT
CUBE	DESTROY	EXTERNAL
CURRENT	DESTRUCTOR	EXTRACT
CURRENT_DATE	DETERMINISTIC	FALSE
CURRENT_PATH	DIAGNOSTICS	FETCH
CURRENT_ROLE	DICTIONARY	FILE
CURRENT_TIME	DISCONNECT	FILLFACTOR
CURRENT_TIMESTAMP	DISK	FIRST
CURRENT_USER	DISTINCT	FLOAT

FOR	IN	LEVEL
FOREIGN	INCLUDE	LIKE
FORTRAN	INDEX	LIMIT
FOUND	INDICATOR	LINENO
FREE	INITIALIZE	LOAD
FREETEXT	INITIALLY	LOCAL
FREETEXTTABLE	INNER	LOCALTIME
FROM	INOUT	LOCALTIMESTAMP
FULL	INPUT	LOCATOR
FULLTEXTTABLE	INSENSITIVE	LOWER
FUNCTION	INSERT	MAP
GENERAL	INT	MATCH
GET	INTEGER	MAX
GLOBAL	INTERSECT	MIN
GO	INTERVAL	MINUTE
GOTO	INTO	MODIFIES
GRANT	IS	MODIFY
GROUP	ISOLATION	MODULE
GROUPING	ITERATE	MONTH
HAVING	JOIN	NAMES
HOLDLOCK	KEY	NATIONAL
HOST	KILL	NATURAL
HOUR	LANGUAGE	NCHAR
IDENTITY	LARGE	NCLOB
IDENTITY_INSERT	LAST	NEW
IDENTITYCOL	LATERAL	NEXT
IF	LEADING	NO
IGNORE	LEFT	NOCHECK
IMMEDIATE	LESS	NONCLUSTERED

NONE	PARAMETER	REFERENCES
NOT	PARAMETERS	REFERENCING
NULL	PARTIAL	RELATIVE
NULLIF	PASCAL	REPLICATION
NUMERIC	PATH	RESTORE
OBJECT	PERCENT	RESTRICT
OCTET_LENGTH	PLAN	RESULT
OF	POSITION	RETURN
OFF	POSTFIX	RETURNS
OFFSETS	PRECISION	REVOKE
OLD	PREFIX	RIGHT
ON	PREORDER	ROLE
ONLY	PREPARE	ROLLBACK
OPEN	PRESERVE	ROLLUP
OPENDATASOURCE	PRIMARY	ROUTINE
OPENQUERY	PRINT	ROW
OPENROWSET	PRIOR	ROWCOUNT
OPENXML	PRIVILEGES	ROWGUIDCOL
OPERATION	PROC	ROWS
OPTION	PROCEDURE	RULE
OR	PUBLIC	SAVE
ORDER	RAISERROR	SAVEPOINT
ORDINALITY	READ	SCHEMA
OUT	READS	SCOPE
OUTER	READTEXT	SCROLL
OUTPUT	REAL	SEARCH
OVER	RECONFIGURE	SECOND
OVERLAPS	RECURSIVE	SECTION
PAD	REF	SELECT

SEQUENCE	TABLE	UPDATETEXT
SESSION	TEMPORARY	UPPER
SESSION_USER	TERMINATE	USAGE
SET	TEXTSIZE	USE
SETS	THAN	USER
SETUSER	THEN	USING
SHUTDOWN	TIME	VALUE
SIZE	TIMESTAMP	VALUES
SMALLINT	TIMEZONE_HOUR	VARCHAR
SOME	TIMEZONE_MINUTE	VARIABLE
SPACE	TO	VARYING
SPECIFIC	TOP	VIEW
SPECIFICTYPE	TRAILING	WAITFOR
SQL	TRAN	WHEN
SQLCA	TRANSACTION	WHENEVER
SQLCODE	TRANSLATE	WHERE
SQLERROR	TRANSLATION	WHILE
SQLEXCEPTION	TREAT	WITH
SQLSTATE	TRIGGER	WITHOUT
SQLWARNING	TRIM	WORK
START	TRUE	WRITE
STATE	TRUNCATE	WRITETEXT
STATEMENT	TSEQUAL	YEAR
STATIC	UNDER	ZONE
STATISTICS	UNION	
STRUCTURE	UNIQUE	
SUBSTRING	UNKNOWN	
SUM	UNNEST	
SYSTEM_USER	UPDATE	

Index

C

DISABLE TRIGGER statement, 246

disabling accounts, 282

DISTINCT argument, 98

DISTINCT keyword, 32

downloading SQL Server, 292

DROP command, stored procedures, 227-228

DROP FULLTEXT, 161

DROP LOGIN statement, 282

DROP statement, syntax, 306

DROP TABLE statement, 197-198

DROP TRIGGER statement, 245

dropping database objects, 306

duplicate rows, deleting, 153-154

E

ELEMENTS keyword, 263

empty strings, compared to NULL values, 190

ENABLE TRIGGER statement, 246

enabling

accounts, 282

full-text searching, 159

encoding character sets, 269-270

equality operator (=), 47

equijoins, 131. *See also* joins

evaluation, order of, 55-57

event triggers, 243, 250

applying, 247-249

assigning, 246

creating, 244-245

dropping, 245

enabling/disabling, 246

example tables

creating, 300-301

customers table, 297-298

orderitems table, 298-299

orders table, 298

overview of, 295-296

productnotes table, 299

products table, 297

vendors table, 296

Execute button, 16

EXECUTE statement, 225

EXISTS statement, 119-121

Exp() function, 89

explicit commits, 255

explicit control, wildcard matching, 158

EXPLICIT mode, 263

Extensible Markup Language. *See* XML

F

FETCH statement

accessing cursors, 239

cursors, 238-240, 242

fields, 70. *See also* columns

calculated

applying subqueries to create, 116-118

concatenating fields, 70-74

mathematical calculations, 75-77

overview, 69-70

views, 205-207

columns, 8

G

INSERT statement and, 178

joins

  aggregate functions, 145-146

  applying, 125-126

  conditions, 147

  creating, 126-127

  inner, 131-132

  multiple tables, 132-134

  overview of, 123

  relational tables, 123-125

  types of, 138, 140-141, 143-144

  WHERE clauses, 128-131

multiple columns, 39-40

multiple WHERE clauses, 152

names, 29

results, 37-39

subqueries

  creating calculated fields, 116-118

  filtering, 111-115

  overview of, 111

  testing with EXISTS, 119-121

table aliases, 138

unsorted data results, 28

views, 199

wildcards, 31

quotes

  applying, 166

  numeric values, 312

  string values, 311

  variables, 216

quotes ("), WHERE clause, 49

R

Rand() function, 89

ranges, WHERE clause, 50

ranking search results, 169-170

REAL datatype, 312

records, 9

referential integrity, maintaining, 126

reformatting retrieved data with views, 203-204

relational databases, 38

relational tables, 123-125

renaming

  logins, 283

  tables, 198

Replace() function, 81

requirements, 291-292

reserved words, 20, 315-319

restrictions, views, 201

results

  queries, 37-39

  ranking search, 169-170

  SELECT statements, 33-35

  sets, 235

retrieving

  aggregate functions

    applying, 99

    Avg(), 92-93

X-Z

REGISTER THIS BOOK

Register this book and unlock benefits exclusive to the owners of this book.

Registration benefits can include

- Additional content
- Book errata
- Source code, example files, and other downloads
- Increased membership discounts
- Discount coupons
- A chance to sign up to receive content updates, information on new editions, and more

Book registration is free and takes only a few easy steps:

1. Go to **www.samspublishing.com/register**
2. Enter the book's ISBN (found above the barcode on the back of your book).
3. You will be prompted to either register for or log in to samspublishing.com.
4. Once you have completed your registration or log in, you will be taken to your "My Registered Books" page.
5. This page will list any benefits associated with each title you register, including links to content and coupon codes.

The benefits of book registration vary with each book, so be sure to register every Sams Publishing book you own to see what else you might unlock at **www.samspublishing.com/register**

Sams Teach Yourself

When you only have time
for the answers™

Whatever your need and whatever your time frame, there's a Sams **Teach Yourself** book for you. With a Sams **Teach Yourself** book as your guide, you can quickly get up to speed on just about any new product or technology—in the absolute shortest period of time possible. Guaranteed.

Learning how to do new things with your computer shouldn't be tedious or time-consuming. Sams **Teach Yourself** makes learning anything quick, easy, and even a little bit fun.

Regular Expressions in 10 Minutes

Ben Forta
ISBN-10: 0-672-32566-7
ISBN-13: 978-0-672-32566-3

Other Sams Teach Yourself in 10 Minutes Titles

Unix in 10 Minutes, Second Edition

Robert Shimonski
ISBN-10: 0-672-32764-3
ISBN-13: 978-0-672-32764-3

SQL in 10 Minutes

Ben Forta
ISBN-10: 0-672-32567-5
ISBN-13: 978-0-672-32567-0

C++ in 10 Minutes, Second Edition

Jesse Liberty
Mark Cashman
ISBN-10: 0-672-32425-3
ISBN-13: 978-0-672-32425-3

Sams **Teach Yourself**

Microsoft®
SQL Server T-SQL

in **10 Minutes**

Sams Teach Yourself Microsoft SQL Server T-SQL in 10 Minutes offers straightforward, practical answers when you need fast results. By working through 10-minute lessons, you'll learn everything you need to know to take advantage of Microsoft SQL Server's T-SQL language.

This handy pocket guide starts with simple data retrieval and moves on to more complex topics, including the use of joins, subqueries, full text-based searches, functions and stored procedures, cursors, triggers, table constraints, XML, and much more.

You'll learn what you need to know methodically, systematically, and simply—in highly focused lessons designed to make you immediately and effortlessly productive.

Tips point out shortcuts and solutions

Cautions help you avoid common pitfalls

Notes explain additional concepts, and provide additional information

Category: Databases/Microsoft SQL Server
Covers: Microsoft SQL Server T-SQL
User Level: Beginning–Intermediate

ISBN-13: 978-0-672-32867-1
ISBN-10: 0-672-32867-4

5 1 9 9 9

9 780672 328671

$19.99 USA / $22.99 CAN / £10.99 Net UK

10 minutes is all you need to learn how to...

- Use T-SQL in the Microsoft SQL Server environment
- Construct complex T-SQL statements using multiple clauses and operators
- Filter data so you get the information you need quickly
- Retrieve, sort, and format database contents
- Join two or more related tables
- Make SQL Server work for you with globalization and localization
- Create subqueries to pinpoint your data
- Automate your workload with triggers
- Create and alter database tables
- Work with views, stored procedures, and more

Register your book at
www.samsp
register to
and source

SAMS

www.samspublishing.com

$3.99

248099
d94–
395–0

No Exchange
Media
Books